A BIT OF GRIT ON HAYSTACKS

A celebration of Wainwright

Contributors

Ann Bowker
Robin N Campbell
A Harry Griffin
Val Hamilton
David McVey
W R Mitchell
Ronald Turnbull
Graham Wilson

Illustrator

Craig Smillie

Edited by Dave Hewitt

A BIT OF GRIT ON HAYSTACKS

A celebration of Wainwright

'And if you, dear reader, should get a bit of grit in your boot as you are crossing Haystacks in the years to come, please treat it with respect. It might be me.'

A Wainwright, *Fellwanderer*

Millrace

First published in Great Britain in 2004 by
Millrace
2a Leafield Road, Disley
Cheshire SK12 2JF
www.millracebooks.co.uk

ISBN: 1 902173 171

Typeset in Adobe Garamond Pro
Produced in the United Kingdom
by LPPS Ltd, Wellingborough, Northants NN8 3PJ

Acknowledgements

The editor wishes to thank all the contributors for their expertise and enthusiasm. Special thanks go to Ann Bowker: in addition to providing one of the pieces for the book, she allowed photographs from her website (www. madaboutmountains.com) to be used as the basis for Craig Smillie's drawings. Thanks are also due to Tom Waghorn for a good idea, to Alan Castle for information on those who have climbed all 214 of Wainwright's fells, to Hunter Davies, whose *Wainwright—The Biography* (Michael Joseph, 1995) is mentioned by several contributors, to Viv Cripps for being a faultless publisher, and to the Carroll family of Coniston for all kinds of help and hospitality. Particular thanks are due to Tessa Carroll, who not only read through the manuscript but also endured the production-process moods and disappearing acts that accompany being shacked up with an editor.

DH

Contents

Contents

Cairns, crags and a cascade of detail
Fifty years of the Pictorial Guide

 As this book goes to press, late in 2004, two connected anniversaries loom. The start of 2007—17 January 2007 to be precise—will mark exactly one hundred years since a man who was to become an outwardly shy northern-English civil servant was born in Blackburn, Lancashire. And the spring of 2005, sometime in late May, will mark fifty years since that same shy civil servant received from the printer copies of the first of the books which would make him famous.

He was Alfred Wainwright, and that first book was entitled *A Pictorial Guide to the Lakeland Fells, Book One, The Eastern Fells*. It is by those final three words, *The Eastern Fells*, that the book tends to be known, just as its six successors are known as *The Far Eastern Fells*, *The Central Fells*, *The Southern Fells*, *The Northern Fells*, *The North Western Fells* and *The Western Fells*. Wainwright went on to write upwards of

1

fifty other books, but it is on those initial seven rucksack-pocket-sized volumes that his reputation rests.

There has been nothing quite like the *Pictorial Guide*, and few other creative works concerning the British hills have come close to emulating its success. On the one hand Wainwright's idea—to document, by drawing and by written word, the uplands of Lakeland—was beautifully simple; on the other hand it was absurdly ambitious. And such was his achievement that the two anniversaries, of birth and of first publication, deserve to be marked in some way. Hence what you have here is a *Festschrift*, a book in celebration of Wainwright's work—although it is a matter of contention what a man with a tendency towards gruffness might have made of such a high-flown foreign word. He would also have grumbled about the fuss (he wrote that he could 'work up no enthusiasm at all' for posterity); but quietly, to himself, he might have felt pleased to see his handiwork acknowledged.

Whatever: *Festschrift* it is, and the various essays that follow cover a wide range of Wainwright's work: memoirs of Wainwright the man, discussion of his on-page artwork and on-fell route-choices, analysis and assessment of the books he went on to write after the first celebrated seven. There are also two pieces directly concerned with inspiration: how Wainwright's guidebooks proved the highlight and salvation of a 1970s summer job in Wasdale; and how, in a different, faster, age they served as the starting-point for that most newfangled and unWainwrightean of things, a website.

What remains striking about the first seven books is how complete they feel, how well the component parts—route-descriptions, incidental asides, ridge and crag drawings, maps, summit panoramas—complement each other on the page. The term 'busy' is used in the world of design to describe pages in magazines, newspapers or books where a clutter of items is crammed together uneasily, discordantly. Wainwright's pages routinely run that risk, but they rarely feel crammed, and it's hard to think of a single busy page in any of his books. At that level, never mind the content, the *Pictorial Guide* is a work of instructive, elegant, lasting genius.

The series occupied Wainwright for thirteen years, and is remarkable in its consistency. There is undoubtedly a degree of development throughout the books—it would be impossible for such a lengthy series not to evolve in some way—but the changes all

appear to have been for the better. As Robin Campbell notes in his essay on the drawings, Wainwright was in control of his art right from the start: he knew what he wanted, and how to achieve it. He immediately displayed a wonderful eye for line and composition, the equivalent of a singer with perfect pitch, or a batsman capable of playing cover drives from the moment he arrives at the crease.

Campbell also mentions Wainwright's relative weakness when drawing skies and water, and notes that the instances of these were reduced in the later guidebooks. Similarly, Book One, *The Eastern Fells*, included thumbnail hill pictures round the rim of his summit panoramas—see, for instance, Catstycam 7 and 8. (Just as the *Pictorial Guide* had no truck with formal typesetting, so orthodox page-numbering was abandoned—to, it scarcely needs to be said, extremely good effect.) These thumbnails didn't really work, and added nothing to the overall design, so Wainwright quietly dropped them when it came to Book Two.

The slight weaknesses, however, were more than offset by his great strengths. The full-page hill-and-valley pictures rarely fail to impress, and has there ever been such an able portrayer of cairns, crags or flowing water? He also excelled at buildings and structures—*The Northern Fells* contains several fine examples of these. Overall, the excellence is such, and so lacking in ostentation, that the reader risks taking it for granted. Turn, for example, to the drawing of the triangulation pillar and cairn on Skiddaw 22. This is never going to be regarded as one of Wainwright's great drawings—it's no Dow Crag 12 or High Stile 2. There is nothing spectacular about the viewpoint and the content borders on the mundane. But it's hard to fault the picture. It does its job effectively and unobtrusively, and there are dozens upon dozens of other drawings—indeed whole complex, composed pages —of which this could be said.

It is also easy to overlook what an accomplished

writer Wainwright was. Again nothing spectacular—
he's never showy, nor is he likely to be considered one
of the great evokers of hills by way of prose. There
is no doubt that drawing and design were his chief
skills. But his writing was quietly effective, and the
occasions when he strayed toward the purple or the
pretentious (eg the 'Soliloquy' on Scafell Pike 24)
were rare. Modern guidebook writers please note.
It helped that Wainwright came from an era when
unfussy, efficient writing was much more common
than now. Ditto the ability to structure a sentence
and to spell. The nearest thing to a spelling mistake in
Wainwright's guides could be when he describes coni-
fers as 'dam prickly' (Latrigg 4); but even that might
simply have been the custom of the time, rather than
a misapprehension.

There isn't space here to fully discuss how Wainwright was unafraid of using prose in forthright and
opinionated ways, a bold habit that manifests itself in
strident comments on hill topography (he labels the
Helvellyn range as 'less interesting' than that centred
on Fairfield—against the received wisdom but surely
accurate), in chuntering about map-portrayal of
non-existent paths, or in anger about animal-rights
abuses. There are numerous sarcastic references to

'sportsmen' who kill animals—see Sale Fell 2 in *The North Western Fells*—and those puzzled by Wainwright's decision to donate his vast royalties to animal welfare should consider that, whether they agree with his views or not, he did at least act on the issue which riled him more than any other. 'My hackles rise only when I hear of cruelty to animals,' he was to write in his late-in-life book *Ex-Fellwanderer*.

There is a surprising amount of humour in the *Pictorial Guide*. Although not to everyone's taste (but then what humour is?), the series maintains a consistent, observational comedy of Other People, with a strong strand of self-deprecation woven in. For typical examples turn to Souther Fell 1 and Lank Rigg 7 in *The Northern Fells* and *The Western Fells* respectively, but there are numerous others. If nothing else, this gives the lie to the caricature of Wainwright as Curmudgeonly Northerner. Even his most notorious observation (of a particularly rough-looking rock on Haystacks he wrote 'Some women have faces like that') is only likely to offend those for whom the portrayal of Norah Batty in *Last of the Summer Wine* was likewise to be frowned at.

The presence of one self-portrait (always from side-on or behind) in the main body of each of the guidebooks can also be seen as a form of humour. These walk-on appearances recall those by another celebrated Alfred and increasingly served as a way for Wainwright to poke fun at himself. In the first four books he appears in purely contemplative mode (usually with pipe in mouth or cigarette in hand, this being before such things were deemed un-PC). But seated on Binsey in Book Five (caption: 'Ancient Briton') he resembles a cross between a yokel and a scarecrow. The Book Six Grasmoor picture is of the earlier pensive type, except that with mock pride a label indicates his jacket to be 'Harris tweed'. And the final picture, Yewbarrow 9 at the end of the last book, is openly comic, with a curiously unfinished-looking white cap and a pair of talking sheep.

Whether each of the seven books is a 'masterpiece' is a matter for debate and personal opinion. There is little doubt that the series, taken as a whole, merits that label, but everyone will have their favourite volume, whether for use on the hill or for browsing by the fireside of a dark winter evening. That my own favourite is Book Four, *The Southern Fells*, is not solely because family connections mean I often spend time in that most perfect of fell-villages, Coniston. For me, Books One and Two carry an air of Wainwright finding his feet, of a style still being evolved. See how relatively scant the detail is, both in terms of the drawing and the minutiae of route-description, for the Striding Edge approach to Helvellyn in Book One compared with the welter of detail for similar routes on other fells—Sharp Edge on Blencathra in Book Five, for example, or the almost step-by-step accounts of Jack's Rake and Lord's Rake in Books Three and Four respectively.

By Book Three, *The Central Fells*, Wainwright had found his style, had settled in. But Book Three suffers from curious topography, in that the Lakeland

Blencathra from
Low Brandlehow

fells, like a certain brand of peppermint sweet, have a hole in the middle. Hence, of the twenty-seven Book Three fells, only High Raise reaches the 2500ft mark, and then only just. The next 'lowest' book is *The Far Eastern Fells*, high-point High Street, 2718ft. This is a substantial difference, and it shows. Even though *The Central Fells* includes the Langdale Pikes and that most celebrated of little fells, Loughrigg, there is a sense of it being the runt of the litter. This is not just because of its page-count—260 pages including endpapers compared with 300 pages or more for each of the other six books—but because it includes more than the standard share of fells which even those with a fair amount of Lakeland knowledge would struggle to place. High Tove, anyone?

The four books that follow, however, are chunky, solid affairs, with Wainwright's now-established style applied to the grand arc of western and northern ridges. *The Western Fells* feels a particularly strong choice for a finishing book, and Wainwright does a fine job of blending its major summits (Gable, Pillar, High Stile) with the smaller treats (Mellbreak, Yewbarrow and his beloved Haystacks). Such is the success of these later books that a case could have been made for Wainwright to revisit the start of the series. This never happened, and it would be wrong to see the first two books as failures—they're still far more accomplished than pretty much any non-Wainwrightean guidebook. But I'm surely not alone in wishing that Helvellyn, in particular, could have been portrayed using the almost forensic level of detail of which Wainwright had shown himself capable by Book Seven.

The sequencing of the books raises another issue, the only aspect of the *Pictorial Guide* where it could be argued that Wainwright lost the plot somewhat. At first glance the distribution of the fells in each of the books seems straightforward, and walkers have become so accustomed to the Wainwright-decreed arrangement that it seems sacrilegious to suggest alterations. Various of the books fit the topographical boundaries perfectly. There is no doubt, for instance, that the Thirlmere-Grasmere road over Dunmail Raise forms a logical divide, and the only real question with regard to the western edge of *The Eastern Fells* is whether to include or exclude High Rigg. (Wainwright drew his line down St John's in the Vale and placed High Rigg in *The Central Fells*.) The Ullswater-Kirkstone valley is another obvious split, and it's right that *The Far Eastern Fells* starts here. *The Northern Fells* is similarly clear-cut, covering the area north of the modern A66 (although a case could be made for transferring the seven small north-of-Whinlatter fells—Lord's Seat, Barf, etc—from *The North Western Fells*).

So far, so straightforward. But Book Four, *The Southern Fells*, for all its undoubted strengths, is a curiosity in terms of content. Again the road system seems to provide a 'natural' boundary: the neat west-east line of the Hardknott and Wrynose passes. To the south of this is without doubt 'southern' in Lakeland terms, so *The Southern Fells* was always going to include the Coniston massif, along with Harter Fell across the Duddon. But *The Southern Fells* doesn't stop at Hardknott-Wrynose: nineteen of its thirty summits lie north of the passes, reaching as far as Rosthwaite Fell above Borrowdale. This lies north of two-thirds of the Central Fells: a considerable overlap.

From High Rigg

Smillie

Wainwright himself was aware of the problem, and in the 'Classification and Definition' section at the start of each book he wrote this: 'Any attempt to define internal or external boundaries is certain to invite criticism, and he who takes it upon himself to say where Lakeland starts and finishes, or, for example, where the Central Fells merge into the Southern Fells and *which* fells *are* the Central Fells and which the Southern and *why* they need to be so classified, must not expect his pronouncements to be generally accepted.'

This serves as a challenge to suggest Boundary Commission-type changes, and looking at the series as a whole it seems that Southern could lose Pike o' Blisco, Bowfell, the Crinkles and Hard Knott to Central, and the Scafells and Illgill Head to Western, thus allowing Hardknott-Wrynose to become the book boundary it cries out to be. But the heartland isn't where the problem makes itself felt, as whether Glaramara is treated as Southern or Central, and Lingmell Southern or Western, is of no real consequence. Such fells were never going to be excluded from the canon—the debate was merely about what book they appeared in. What the Southern Fells overload did do, however, was to crop the true southern end of Lakeland to such an extent that those who make 'pronouncements' on this are unlikely to define things the way Wainwright did.

The Southern Fells ends abruptly, the southern limit being the top of the Walna Scar Pass, cutting across the south ridge of Dow Crag at a height which Wainwright gave as 1995ft. Here he brings the curtain down on the edge of his *Pictorial Guide* universe, yet to stand in the pass with this in mind is akin to the moment in *The Truman Show* when Jim Carrey sails his yacht straight into the painted wall that marks the edge of the TV studio and, by definition, his world. There are interesting-looking hills immediately south of the Walna Scar Pass. Walna Scar itself and White Maiden both top the 2000ft contour, while White Pike is a fine peak with a steep south-western face. But Wainwright had no truck with these, at least not until the reluctant 1974 afterthought of his *Outlying Fells* book, because *The Southern Fells*, at 340 pages, was already full to overflowing. The consequence of including Rosthwaite Fell and its north-of-Wrynose neighbours (including the distinctly unsouthern Scafells) was to create a knock-on effect where the deep south never got a look-in beyond an uneasy footnote on Dow Crag 2. Here Wainwright claimed that the missing 2000ers, along with Caw and Stickle Pike, lay 'beyond the boundary of fellwalking country'. This reads as a fudge—there is, after all, no material difference between Buck Pike and White Maiden to either side of the Walna Scar Pass—and Wainwright surely knew it.

So where else could the southern boundary have been drawn? It's hard to be certain, but craggy Caw has as much right to be a Lakeland insider as do the bumps of Great Mell Fell and Little Mell Fell, both of which merit chapters in *The Eastern Fells*. A true southern book could even go the whole distance and take in the much-loved Black Combe, a terminal Lakeland fell without question.

That isn't what happened, though. Wainwright drew his line where he did, and his southern limit will have this same abrupt feel for evermore. He must have known that an eighth book—*The Far Southern Fells*, perhaps—would have made sense. But with his eye for balance and elegance, his intuitive understanding of the Golden Section and other such devices, he would also have regarded it as inescapable that whereas the series could comprise the mystical total of seven books, the prosaic and mundane eight would have been out of the question. And fair enough: it was, ultimately, his decision. As far as his guidebooks were concerned, he was the boss, the benign dictator.

Anyway, enough of that. Just a couple of other thoughts before the essayists are let loose on their subject. It has been suggested that the popularity of Wainwright's work has proved self-defeating, in that it encourages so many people on to the Lakeland fells that the area's essential away-from-it-all-ness has been lost. Twaddle. There is no doubt that the fells are busier than other major UK hill ranges (with the exception of Snowdonia—which has never known the Wainwright level of depiction). The hills of Torridon, Glen Coe, the Cairngorms or the Cuillin are markedly quieter, but surely the reasons for this are geographical and socio-industrial. The proximity of cities means that far more people live within an hour or two's journey of the Lakes than is the case with all but the southern fringe of the Scottish Highlands. And the rise of the relatively well-off middle-classes, with their leisure time and their motor cars, is a far weightier factor than the long-ago evening- and weekend-work of a reclusive borough treasurer.

To blame Wainwright for over-thronged fells feels

like a bad case of shooting the messenger. Donald McGill's saucy seaside postcards might as well be held culpable for the modern sex industry. The busyness and the erosion of the Cumbrian uplands were always going to happen, and one man's work is neither here nor there in this. And anyway, what's wrong with hills being busy? There will always be quiet corners between the main paths, and too often the hills-should-be-empty zealots sound like straightforward elitists. What they really mean is that the hills should be empty *apart from them*. Well, tough. The hills, almost by definition, are for everyone. Wainwright knew this better than most and was more egalitarian than elitist: at the end of Book One he noted that if his work brought people to the hills 'I shall be well pleased'. So if someone doesn't like seeing other people on the slopes then they have two options: find some quieter, off-path hillside, or stay at home and fester.

Indeed, if this book helps to renew people's acquaintance with the *Pictorial Guide*, and to introduce a few newcomers to the fold and to the fells, then that's as it should be. Wainwright's work has been in print for fifty years, and it's to be hoped that this will continue for at least another fifty. Other authors have tried to follow in the great man's footsteps, with varying degrees of success (Bill Birkett's *Complete Lakeland Fells* is the pick of the post-Wainwright bunch), but there's still not much wrong with the original and best.

There is a view that the most appropriate way to use a hill guidebook is to ignore it until the walk has been done, thus maintaining, at least in part, the spirit of adventure. Either that, or—and this is an indictment of the way in which guidebooks corridorise paths and cause walkers to cluster rather than to seek out space and solitude—to consult the book ahead of the walk as a method of working out where *not* to go. If the guidebook recommends Ridge A (busy, possibly a bit dull), then the route to try is Valley B (quiet, interesting). Happily, this doesn't apply when it comes to Wainwright, because his *Pictorial Guide*, with its multifarious routes, its cascade of detail, is so much more than just a series of seven guidebooks. The man who laboured long and lovingly over this was a true adventurer, and his legacy offers near-infinite scope for striding out along breezy ridges, or rummaging around in neglected, rock-choked corners.

So if you don't already own a set of the *Pictorial Guide*, go out and find one. Either the current, inprint edition or, better still, a dog-eared second-hand set, as the hot-metal print and the slightly faded paper undoubtedly add to the overall pleasure. Then dig out a rucksack, lace on a pair of boots, and maybe secrete a compass about your person, even though Wainwright himself had no time for such devices. And then, without further ado, head to the fells for the good of your soul. Oh, and as the old, shy civil servant himself never tired of saying, watch where you're putting your feet.

Solo walks and evening work
Wainwright remembered

Wainwright came into my life half a century ago when Harry Firth, printer, arrived at the *Dalesman* office in north-west Yorkshire with a small packet which he reverently unwrapped. Into view came what are now the familiar hand-written, hand-drawn pages of a walker's guide to the eastern fells. In the mid-1950s, this had novelty value. I marvelled at the meticulous penmanship of a book that was intended to be printed with the pages as they were, with none of the customary sub-editing or proof-reading. Harry Firth mentioned that the author-artist was a Mr Wainwright—those were respectful days. This Mr Wainwright presided over the finance department at Kendal town hall and what I looked at was evening work, spread over two years.

As I looked at the pages of an astonishing first book, I could not have foreseen that a series of seven would be produced. Or that by the year 1986 over one million copies of Wainwright's guides would have been sold. Because *Dalesman* and *Cumbria* were printed by the same firm in Kendal, I became familiar with white cliffs of printed sheets. Over 200 tons of paper had been used for those million copies.

I gathered that Wainwright—simply AW to his close friends—was a character. He was a man of original thought and action who recoiled from the idea of personal publicity. Harry Firth, for whom he had a great regard, arranged a meeting early in 1955. I duly turned up in Wainwright's office, having entered the town hall from a side door, to be confronted by a tall, bespectacled man wearing a suit of a quiet shade that had absorbed the tang of pipe tobacco. He spoke quietly and was sparing with his words. Grasping notebook and pencil, I awaited an opportunity to start the interview. When I mentioned my joy at having seen some of his work, he fumbled in a desk drawer and brought out other examples. Another pause, then he did not allow the interview to take place. I faced not so much a refusal as a process of being bogged down with petty details, such as how many words I would write and how long it would take me.

I suggested that I might submit some questions to him by post, with a stamped addressed envelope for his considered reply. He agreed, and at home he dutifully set down his answers. They were never posted. Hunter Davies, his eventual biographer, found the questionnaire and the replies when he sifted through papers made available by Betty, AW's widow. Davies presumed that AW had sent a copy to me, as he had written his replies at length. His observations appeared in the biography, and from these it seemed that AW always had a passion for hillwalking, even when a small boy. Other enthusiasms had come and gone, but his love of the fells remained constant. Having been inspired by the 2½-inch Ordnance Survey maps, which had just been republished at

that time, AW had decided to make his own up-to-date maps, his own diagrams, his own drawings, all carefully designed and presented as attractively as he could. I had asked in my questionnaire if he always walked alone. His answer was 'invariably … I should be a poor companion, for my walks must often seem to be erratic…'

AW revealed that as things were not going well with sales of *The Eastern Fells*, he was ready to agree to anything to get a bit more publicity. In due course, the two magazines I edited came to his help. With Harry Firth as a go-between, I was able to use a page from a Wainwright book in each issue of each magazine, which alerted a total of around 90,000 readers a month. There were readers in almost every country, many of them nostalgic for their home acres.

Wainwright, I discovered, had penned the first page of what would become the celebrated series on the evening of 9 November 1952. 'At that time I had no thought of publication,' he was to recall. 'I was working for my own pleasure and enjoying it hugely.' He carried the venture to a breathtaking conclusion at the rate of one page an evening for thirteen years, latterly in the company of Totty, his favourite cat. How he managed to work so patiently and meticulously, and to keep to the style he fixed from the start, is explained by his profession—that of accountant, where vagueness and impetuosity are not tolerated. He did have a dash of romance in his nature, however. On drawing pictures of the lake-country, using Indian ink on substantial paper, he rejoiced in being able to build a mountain on a blank sheet. 'Let's do Great Gable as seen from Lingmell,' he might say. The guides became an obsession.

✒ ✒ ✒

There had been an unsatisfactory start. When, in July 1953, Wainwright had prepared a hundred pages of pictures and prose, he scrapped them because he did not like the raggedness of the line-ends. They were not 'justified', to use a printing term. He did the work again, fitting the lines as neatly as he could make them. 'I never quite succeeded but the pages looked better than before. They were neater and tidier.' There followed 'a dreamlike procession of happy, uneventful days ... I never had an accident or a fall. I was never be-nighted in a blizzard nor tossed by a bull ... I always walked alone.' He apparently never had a compass. Using public transport where possible, he carried an old-fashioned mac and wore nailed boots.

His work of recording the shape and character of the fells was made possible through photography, with a second-hand camera.

When Harry Firth showed me the original artwork of Wainwright's first guide, he mentioned the author's alarm when £950 was quoted as the cost of printing 2000 copies. Wainwright had only £35 to his name. His reputation was such, however, that he was allowed to pay for the work when the copies had been sold. He did pay, but it took him two years, during which he was never once reminded of the debt. Having little experience of publishing, Wainwright asked a good friend, Henry Marshall, the Kendal librarian, to distribute and despatch copies of the first guide. Henry's name thus appeared on the title page of the first edition—and, incidentally, it was to him that I went for consolation and help when my interview with AW failed.

As the first commercial arrangement collapsed through weight of numbers, Wainwright was left with the task of keeping records, sending out invoices and collecting money—as well as writing more books. He was relieved when, in 1963, the *Westmorland Gazette* took over their publication. Harry Firth, as manager of the printing department, became his mentor and friend. As Harry Firth was also numbered among my friends, I had copies of the Wainwright guides hot from the press.

Wainwright devoted most evenings to his guides but broke off for half-an-hour twice a week to watch *Coronation Street*, as this reminded him of his upbringing in Blackburn. He recalled the period in *Fellwanderer* (1966), mentioning flickering gas lamps, hot-potato carts, fish-and-chip shops, public houses and Saturday matinees at the cinema known, not without justification, as 'the flea-pit'. A glimpse of those days was given to me by Helen Lund (née Smith), a first cousin of AW, who remembered him from the days when she stayed with her Auntie Emily, AW's mother, at their red-brick terrace home, 331 Audley Range, during summer holidays. At dinner-time, she saw a tall, red-haired lad arrive for a meal. AW was married, with a young child. He worked at the town hall and lived in a new estate at the edge of town. It was handier for him to drop in on mother for dinner. Helen Lund recalled that he was pleasant enough but taciturn. 'He'd just say "Hello" and "Good-bye"—and that was that.'

Helen also recalled that Auntie Emily 'was a saint if ever I knew one. She was a bonnie woman, quite small, of average build, with reddish cheeks.' She was grey-haired when Helen first knew her. AW's father, Albert, was a master mason, charming when sober but garrulous and coarse when drunk. We have AW's own account of this lack of harmony in his home background. Emily was left to take in washing, a common enough occupation of married women in the old milltowns, and AW was to recall with sadness his waking during the night and hearing the mangle being operated.

He left school at the age of thirteen, having little in the way of learning. If he wanted to 'get on', he must pass examinations. So he studied English and literature, which made him a stickler for the correct use of language. His early hillwalking was in the Bowland and Pendle areas, which were handy from town. Not until 1930, when he was twenty-three years old, did he visit the Lake District. He described himself at that time as shy, sensitive, skinny, ungainly, having a crop of red hair and wearing glasses. 'I had saved £5 for a week off. It was the first time I had ever been away from home. I went with a friend [his cousin, Eric Beardsall] to see the Lakes I had heard people talk about. It was the moment that changed my life. I was absolutely captivated.' Helen Lund recalled both men as being quiet. 'I suppose they walked in silence all the way.'

Subsequently, when AW began his series of guidebooks, the service buses were his transport as he toured the district. He stayed at bed-and-breakfast houses, where the charge was four shillings a night. At first he walked in everyday clothes, with stout shoes on his feet. He carried a raincoat. Then he wore a good jacket and was shod in ex-Army nailed boots. Lakeland excursions became much easier in 1941, when he obtained a post in the borough treasurer's office at Kendal. (He would serve as borough treasurer from 1948 until 1967.)

Wainwright was a strong, solitary, silent character. He did not care much for his Christian name, Alfred, considering that although it was nice for a small boy it was not very manly. In early life, shyness made him a recluse. When his achievements as a local government officer and guidebook writer gave him assurance, he still preferred his own company to that of a crowd. He had several good friends, but 'people in the mass mean nothing to me.' Another time, he observed: 'I do not like the stage; my place is out of sight in the wings.' On seeing a crocodile of schoolchildren on a footpath, he hid behind a boulder, took another route or, when a meeting was inevitable, passed the time of day with the leading person. That greeting must suffice for them all.

For many years he refused to be photographed. In my files, I had a snap of him in profile, pipe in mouth, shock of grey hair protruding from under his cap—a cap with a neb. Not wishing to upset him by using it in one of the magazines, I would take the picture out of its file at least once a year, sigh, and return it to its snug retreat. The writer John Hillaby, who never met Wainwright, nonetheless described him as 'quirky, querulous, gruff, sometimes to the point of rudeness'. He was said to dislike writing letters. Yet many letters are known to exist, neatly typed, signed in green ink. When I wrote a book about Scotland, AW provided a foreword and subsequently signed several copies.

He 'came out of his shell' a little when, in 1988, he agreed to be interviewed by Sue Lawley for *Desert Island Discs*. He did not intend to travel to London, specifying that the recording should be made in Manchester and that he should be rewarded by a visit to a fish-and-chip shop. Among his choice of music was the appropriately named 'Happy Wanderer'. Instead of a book, he wanted two photographs: one of the cup-winning Blackburn Rovers team of 1928 and the other of Betty.

Some years later, when increasing age and stiff limbs forbade him to take to the hills, and when Bob Swallow and I accompanied his wife for a walk in the Dales, AW stayed in the car, which was parked at Dent along with a goodly number of other vehicles. Dent was beset by tourists. When we returned, hours later, AW was sitting as we had left him. He explained that if he had got out of the car he might have been recognised. That was the day we met a farmer wearing wellingtons, one black, one green. We observed this was unusual. The farmer said: 'Nay—my son's got a pair just t'same.'

To Wainwright, the Lakeland fells held evidence of old-time industry. He was aware of the effort that went into the drystone walls. When several of us began fellwalking regularly as The Geriatric Blunderers, we encountered metal gates, still hung but of no practical value, the wire fences having rusted away. The gates were named after Wainwright and we made a special point of using them—opening and closing them as we thought of the man who inspired our excursions.

AW dedicated his first book to 'the Men of the

Ordnance Survey', the six-inch maps showing the wall patterns and the courses of roads and paths leading to mines and quarries, where 'silence is always more profound in places where once there was noise.' Abandoned sheepfolds fascinated him. Books were dedicated to the stone-wallers, to Lakeland dogs and, of course, to Lakeland sheep. When he took photographs with a camera which had 'various contrivances', all that concerned him was how to put in a new film and 'which knob to press to take a picture'. In his rendering of the fells, his aim was to draw them as they were. The romantic side of his nature led him to write that 'it is the bewitching beauty of Lakeland

Latrigg

that haunts the mind, as the daffodils of Ullswater haunted Wordsworth: scenes that pass across the inward eye as a pageant of loveliness.'

Wainwright liked to be solitary but did not enjoy the lonely years after the collapse of his first marriage. When Betty, his second wife, first knew him, he was subsisting on a standing order at the grocer's, augmented by liberal helpings of shop-bought fish and chips. In 1986, he went public via television programmes that were apt to impair the legend. AW was not an especially good broadcaster, and the BBC had frequently to cope with gloomy wet days, on one of which most of the interview took place indoors.

Having been divorced from their respective spouses in 1968, Alfred and Betty were married at a quiet ceremony in County Hall, Kendal, in March 1970. At an eightieth birthday exhibition at Abbot Hall, Kendal, some of his pens and pipes, also a pair of boots, were among the objects in glass cases. The boots were old-fashioned, inexpensive and well-worn. I saw a pair of his socks on display in a permanent exhibition at Kendal Museum, and at the studio of the sculptor Clive Barnard I viewed a life-sized bust of AW. He had been persuaded to attend a sitting. 'He felt at ease with us,' said the sculptor.

In Lakeland, Wainwright became almost as famous as Wordsworth. 'Doing the Wainwrights', the 214 fells mentioned in his seven main guidebooks, soon became a popular challenge. Up at Wasdale Show, I met Joss Naylor—he who climbed all the Wainwrights in a week. I asked him how he planned it. Joss simply remarked: 'I did a book a day.'

I last met AW at the offices of *Cumbria* magazine. He was eighty years old. We chatted about his interest in and financial support for needy animals, and I suggested that we might go to the Gamecock at Austwick for a bar snack. There was more good-natured chat. On the return, Betty drove to near the village of Clapham, where I left the car, intending to have a short walk back to the office. As the car departed, I saw the head and shoulders of pipe-smoking AW framed in the rear window. That was the last I saw of him.

Wainwright's output over the years was enormous. In addition to his guides, he had produced books about the Pennine Way, the Howgills, the limestone country and his beloved Scottish Highlands. He devised and presented in book form details of my own favourite excursion, the Coast to Coast Walk. A substantial book about old Westmorland—hand-written and drawn—appeared in 1974, when Boundary Commission recommendations absorbed it in the new county of Cumbria. At the age of seventy-eight, he was working on what he was sure would be his last book, to be called *Ex-Fellwanderer* and eventually published to coincide with his eightieth birthday. He intended to reminisce about Lakeland walks, the times he had experienced, and there would be a little bit of philosophising about what is happening to the Lake District. 'Then I will sign off for good.'

He had begun his guidebook project to revive memories of days on the hills when he was too old to climb. Ironically, with fading eyesight, he eventually saw the world as through a mist. On his last true fellwalk, to Haystacks, his eyesight was fading. It was a wet day. 'The mountains wept for me that day; it never stopped raining.' He could not see where he was putting his feet.

Betty scattered his ashes by Innominate Tarn, on Haystacks. Bob Swallow had a theory that before long, most of the ashes would be transferred on the boots of visiting walkers to the bar of the local hostelry. The idea would have appealed to Wainwright, who had

smillie

Innominate Tarn

ended *Fellwanderer* with the words: 'And if you, dear reader, should get a bit of grit in your boot as you are crossing Haystacks in the years to come, please treat it with respect. It might be me.'

Fifty years ago, Wainwright met few people on the high paths of Lakeland. After years of privation, in wartime and its austere aftermath, people with leisure and means were escaping from a mechanised 'progressive' world to areas such as the Lake District, using updated maps on which were the hatched lines signifying rights of way. Wainwright was the champion of the lone walker. He was his most cheerful companion, following his own precept that 'pessimists never reach the top of anything'.

Inevitably, as his guides became bestsellers, he would be blamed by some for the dreadful erosion of the high paths and the way that some fellsides were becoming scree slopes. Wainwright claimed the erosion would have taken place anyway in the rediscovery of the Lakeland landscape. He popularised the Lake District. He was also guilty, now and again, of leading his readers along tracks that were not official, to the vexation of local landowners. Those who had the compulsion to 'do all the Wainwrights' were not going to be put off by any restrictions.

Yet Wainwright transformed our way of looking at the fell country and, by encouraging us to get up and walk, he prolonged our active lives.

VAL HAMILTON

That was Wasdale, that was
On first discovering Wainwright

I know exactly where I was when I read my first Wainwright book: the poky, smoky, viewless staffroom in the eaves of the Wastwater Hotel at Wasdale Head. It was July 1977, the beginning of a formative nine weeks spent working as a chambermaid at the hotel, during which time I learnt a great deal about human nature, blocked urinals and the art of solitary hillwalking.

Much earlier in the year I had answered the advertisement for temporary hotel staff which used to appear regularly in *Climber and Rambler*, but had not received a reply. Then, early in July and threatened with the alternative prospect of a summer at home after a year's freedom at university, I had telephoned to chase my application. This time, the response had been 'come now', so I did.

I became a chambermaid by default, due to my lack of experience in other more skilled tasks such as waitressing or basic cookery. It put me off cleaning for life. The work was tedious and, although physical, was not sufficiently strenuous to give satisfaction. The only exercise for the brain was the weekly preparation of laundry lists, a task I soon took over from the permanent housekeeper, who disliked it. Eventually I realised with naive amazement that she found writing difficult. She surpassed me, however, in all other chores, with a mastery of Nelly the intransigent Nilfisk vacuum cleaner and an ability to spin out or speed up jobs as necessary to fit the hours of work.

By the end of the second day, it was clear that a survival strategy was necessary. This had two elements: acquiring a supply of reading matter, which included nabbing newspapers discarded by residents, and making the most of the special location. Wainwright's books came to combine both these categories.

I now wonder why I had not encountered Wainwright's books before. As a child, I had spent several camping holidays in the Lake District, doing the general touristy things including some gentle walking. The Lakes were popular with my Sheffield student friends, but the emphasis was more on Climbing and Hard Stuff and perhaps Wainwright was regarded as rather tame, even twee. The area did have a literary backdrop for me, firstly through my mother's War Economy Standard Edition Arthur Ransome books. I was no sailor, so my favourites were the land-based stories such as *Pigeon Post* and *Swallowdale*, with their emphasis on maps and hills. Even more appealing were Marjorie Lloyd's *Fell Farm* books which, although written in the 1950s, were in modern Puffin editions and seemed less dated. More importantly, they had real maps with real placenames.

Finding Wainwright's books was a surprise and delight. I was immediately attracted to their small size and the quality of their production. The hotel staffroom copies had lost their dustjackets and so looked more serious, even Bible-like in their muted leather bindings. The illustrations were instantly appealing and so skilful—but, from the start, my favourite sections were the ascent sketches. I enjoyed maps and knew how to navigate, but I was still no good at contours. I understood them, of course, but tended to overlook them, so the pictures showing what I would literally be up against on a particular route were valuable. The panorama-view diagrams, by contrast, seemed mechanical. Even Wainwright hints at the chore involved in constructing them, when a screen of trees on Raven Crag provides 'relief ... for the conscientious chronicler of summit views'. The panoramas meant nothing to me out of context and, once on the summit, the map could be used for identifying peaks until local knowledge filled its place. In any case, the books seemed too fine to take on to the hills. Similarly, despite Wainwright's regular advocacy, I could not consider defacing them by using them 'as basic notebooks' in which readers could make 'their own corrections as the need arises'.

The text fascinated me too, both in form and content. Being neither artistic nor neat, I marvelled at the skill and patience involved in producing such a volume of script. Because my main source was *The Western Fells*, the last in the series, my first impression of the content was of humour, even whimsy—a characteristic not always associated with Wainwright. The first hill I turned to was Kirk Fell where the steep direct ascent from Wasdale Head features the comment: 'Back buttons cannot stand the strain, and wearers of braces are well advised to profit from a sad experience of the author on this climb and take a belt as reserve support.' This is accompanied by a sketch of a cartoon figure looking back between his legs at the 'superb upside-down view of Wasdale Head'.

The route descriptions proved very useful. I had

Smillie   Scoat Fell & Pillar

not thought that I would be walking on my own, as I had expected my fellow workers to be there because of the hills. Some of the permanent staff were walkers or climbers, but the appeal of their surroundings had dimmed long ago. Surprisingly few of the summer contingent were outdoor folk, but there was one notable exception. Ang Phu Sherpa had been on Chris Bonington's two Everest South West Face expeditions and, as a reward for the successful ascent in 1975, Bonington had promised him a trip to the UK. Presumably working as a kitchen porter at the Wastwater was only part of this bonus. Ang Phu was shy, modest and always smiling, and he cooked a wondrous curry for both staff and guests one evening.

He was to reach the summit of Everest in 1978 and again the following year, but died on the descent. Only two years on from our encounter in such gentle and mundane circumstances, his death was hard to comprehend.

There were colleagues I could easily have asked for route suggestions, but I was reluctant to expose my inexperience. It was good therefore to be able to turn to Wainwright for advice. I grew to realise that I could trust his judgement: his perspective was, like mine, that of the 'ordinary common or garden fell walker' (as he wrote of Jack's Rake on Pavey Ark).

Guidebook writers who understate difficulties do their readers no favours. While Wainwright admires, even envies rock climbers, he regards their Easy Gullies with marked caution: 'Rock climbers don't seem to know the meaning of easy,' he wrote of Dow Crag. He might enjoy the ascent of Sergeant Man by a 'rock stairway requiring continuous hand-and-foot climbing', but is reassuringly wary in any situation where 'deviations will end fatally'. (Jack's Rake again.)

Under his influence, my first objective was Pillar which he describes, by the Black Sail route, as 'the easiest way to any of the Wasdale summits. A good walker will do it nonstop.' I had not yet learned to pace myself, a difficult skill which requires self-discipline or years of experience, so I reached the Black Sail Pass quickly. Unfortunately the weather was miserable—raining and windy—and, as my confidence dripped away in the thick cloud, I decided to retreat. This was clearly the sensible thing to do and it was one advantage of not having told anyone where I was going: there was no face to be lost.

For my next day off a week later, I thought I was being less ambitious. I had recently been introduced by Graham, my boyfriend, to the concept that only summits of 2000 feet or more were Real Hills. A large proportion of the hills in Wainwright's books are lower than the magic mark, and this lack of heightism may be regarded as one of the strengths of the books. Wainwright does arrange summits by height in the introductory maps, and altitude is an important criterion in the selection of his best half-dozen fells. But in describing the attractions of Pike o' Blisco, for example, he says 'height alone counts for nothing', and of course Haystacks, 'the best fell-top of all', is a mere 1900 feet. I thought that climbing Illgill Head above Wastwater Screes was a sensibly modest goal at 1983 feet. It was another wet day, but

I enjoyed myself and felt that I had achieved something. Importantly, it gave me the confidence for my first evening summit.

Meals for the hotel staff were excellent: we ate the same food as the guests and in huge quantities. The timing was, however, very compressed. Staff breakfast was served after the guests had finished at around 9.30 am, or later if they lingered, as was often the case on a wet day. Usually I had done three hours of work by then. Dinner was eaten before the guests, at 4.30 pm, which meant hunger pangs mid-evening but did allow several hours to get out on the fells before dark. This was where chambermaiding scored over all the other jobs in the hotel which required working both morning and evening shifts.

smillie

Pillar, Steeple & Scoat Fell from Ennerdale Water

Wainwright comments on the 'unattractive' view of Lingmell's vast wall from the hotel dining-room and the unappealing nature of 'its 2000 feet of unremitting steepness'. But Lingmell's immediacy appealed to me and I stormed up it after tea one evening in seventy-five minutes, feeling really pleased with myself. The views were extensive, and out beyond the chimneys of Sellafield (Calder Hall at the time and, in Wainwright's eyes, 'a blot on the landscape'), a fairytale castle floated in a blue and pink haze over the Irish Sea. I had never seen the Isle of Man before and thought at first it was a mirage or hallucination. It appears that Wainwright did not share my enchantment. His comment, 'some walkers seem to experience a fierce joy in the sight of the Isle of Man in a view,' implies he is not among this group.

Now much more confident, my next day off featured a second attempt on Pillar. Again visibility was poor, but I had more of a feel for my surroundings and capabilities, and this time did not turn back. I continued along the ridge to Steeple and, nearing Haycock, met two runners who greeted me with the phrase, 'I wandered lonely from the cloud.' I felt as though I was becoming part of a club.

The following evening I was out again after tea, this

time on Kirk Fell. I powered up the shortest route from Row Head: 'the most direct ascent in Lakeland ... a relentless and unremitting treadmill, a turf-clutching crawl', and even, having first checked to see there was no one else around, self-consciously performed Wainwright's head-between-the-legs routine—though any excuse to stop was welcome. Again, I had a sense of achievement as I ambled down via Black Sail Pass back to the bar, to mention casually what I had just done.

I had been at Wasdale for four weeks without leaving the valley or its surrounding hills. The self-contained community within the hotel, with its small circle of staff, could feel very claustrophobic, but the isolation had been broken by a surprising number of friends calling in, including several passing through on backpacking trips. There was of course an ever-changing stream of guests, and, while hotel residents did not socialise with the cleaners, there had been plenty of contact with campers and bunkhouse-users in the bar. Staff from the local Outward Bound centre used the billiard room as a comfortable, dry base while they sent clients out to have their characters formed in the cold and rain, and they were as keen to pass the hours chatting as I was.

But I was ready for a change of scene, if not of

company. Planning the Great Escape Expedition involved some serious map-and-book consultation. While Wainwright could give me fine detail of each hill to be visited, the alphabetical layout of the books made it hard to pull together a whole route involving several summits. My self-confidence had still not reached a stage where I was prepared to tell anyone of my ambitious plans, and no one asked where I was going when I set off one morning on the Mountain Goat minibus service which called several times a week. It felt very strange to be going out into a less confined world, down the ten miles of narrow lanes to the end of the valley, then back through Eskdale and over the Hardknott pass to Cockley Beck bridge, which was my chosen starting point. As the bus drove off, I felt nervous. The only way back was over the high fells, and I was propelled by adrenaline up the rough slopes of Little Stand and on to the Crinkles. Fortunately the weather was ideal, with good visibility but not too hot.

By now I was fit after a month of hard work and regular walking. My map-reading abilities were hardly stretched; it was more a question of micronavigation, of choosing the right route beneath my feet. There were plenty of reassuring landmarks as I made my way past the Three Tarns and over the summit of Bowfell, one of Wainwright's top half-dozen fells but just another waymark for me that day. Then it was on to Esk Pike, an important goal, being one of the few Lakeland 2000-foot peaks that boyfriend Graham had not climbed. Only then could I relax, knowing it was downhill all the way, first to Sty Head where I ate a belated lunch, then back to the valley which felt like home. The whole trip had been a challenge, and definitely one of those hill days enjoyed more in retrospect than at the time.

The weather that summer was but a soggy shadow of the glories of 1976 and, after my initial pair of evening ascents, my after-dinner walking had been limited to the valleys and one stroll up to Burnmoor Tarn. But toward the end of August I managed to climb Yewbarrow, undeterred by Wainwright having shed his blood for me on his ascent (see Yewbarrow 6 in *The Western Fells*). Perhaps because Yewbarrow is the last hill in the last book of the series, there is an end-of-term air about the sheep with cartoon bubble comments and his treatise on the merits of 'a tough and rubbery bottom' which, while useless during ascent, is on descending, 'a valuable agent of friction, a sheet anchor with superb resistance to the pull of

Crinkle Crags & Bowfell from Cold Pike   Smillie

gravity.' Neither ascent nor descent caused me problems, apart from the surprise of finding that I was coming down in the dark. Summer was nearly over.

My final walk from Wasdale took me out of the valley again but felt less daunting, as it was a circuit from the hotel door. Wainwright, unlike so many guidebook writers, assumes that normal walkers will want to make a circular tour. On rare occasions he recommends a there-and-back walk, but these are noted as exceptions. I had wanted to visit Ennerdale, so headed over Black Sail Pass, dropping to the youth hostel, then climbed to Scarth Gap for the view over to Buttermere. It would be good to say that my planning skills had improved with my fitness, but I underestimated the amount of climbing this day would involve. I had also failed to take account of the draining power of the wind: this had been strong when I started and worsened during the day. My return took me over Steeple and Red Pike, on a compass bearing in zero visibility with the gale throwing gravel around me. I was sodden but exhilarated by the time I reached Dore Head, where I dropped below the cloud. I had managed to navigate in foul conditions, I knew where I was, and I felt unassailable. But Overbeck was a long wet trudge and, at 4 pm, the weak link in my circular plan was evident. I still had a three-mile road walk, which meant I would miss dinner.

There was nothing to be lost by trying to hitch, although it seemed unlikely anyone would invite such a bedraggled passenger into a clean, dry car. I stuck out a tentative, dripping thumb and, to my amazement, the first car stopped. The couple in it were only going to the campsite a mile up the road but had a son walking in the Dales that week and took pity on me. It did not matter to me that the seats in the back of the estate car were down for their fishing gear and I had to dive in head first and lie prone alongside the rods. They drove me all the way to the hotel in time for tea.

I left Wasdale in early September. On my last evening, I spent a chunk of my earnings—£14.99 a week—in the hotel's outdoor shop, buying mole-skin breeches, a wool balaclava, Dachstein mitts and Alan Hankinson's book, *The First Tigers*, with its photograph of the boot-filled hotel entrance hall and account of the billiard-room traverse. Why no Wainwrights? I don't know, but two summers later Graham bought me the set of seven for my twenty-first birthday. And so, soon after, I married him.

Sheepwalks and sudden death
Wainwright's nasty ways up

 As the title of the present volume suggests, anyone crossing Lakeland in the present century is treading on the ashes of those who have gone before. This applies in particular to Great Gable, a much-favoured ash-scatter spot where the fellrunner Joss Naylor has complained about the stuff getting into his Walsh trainers. Walking and writing in Lakeland, I find I get A Wainwright's grit in my boot rather frequently—and not just on Haystacks. Write about Helvellyn? Wainwright has already described fifteen ways up Helvellyn. Barf? Grike? Great Mell Fell? Alfred's already been at 'em.

Accordingly, as a starting-out outdoor writer in the 1980s I found it was necessary to shake Wainwright out of my socks by not reading his *Pictorial Guide* at all. I did look at him occasionally for his pictures, or if I needed something to argue against. Stuck for something to say about Haycock? Look up *The*

Ennerdale Water & High Crag from Haystacks Summit

Western Fells, see what AW has to say about Haycock ('a giant in stature')—and disagree with it.

Later in life I began to treat Wainwright's 214 fells as a tick-list. Alfred himself would surely have disapproved of this most strongly. Even so, I became grateful to him for tempting me away from Great Gable and up over such minor delights as Fellbarrow and Troutbeck Tongue. Then there's the one that's not a hill at all: Bonscale Pike. It's a point, and not even a high point, on the rim of the damp plateau that tails away in the general direction of Penrith. There are no rational grounds for including Bonscale Pike in any listing of Lakeland. Except that, when you get there, there are. Bonscale Pike is a place in its own right, with a cairn and some rocky grass, that overlooks—indeed, almost overhangs—Ullswater.

And it was thanks to Wainwright that I unrolled my bivvy on Binsey, surrounded by Stone Age stones, with the red light of Aspatria in the east and the last gleams picking out Catbells in the distant south—which was, of course, a piquantly peculiar place to have Catbells.

    🚬 🚬 🚬

Alfred Wainwright was a lamb rather than a lion. Reading between the lines of his 1986 book *A Pennine Journey*, he was nervous and uncomfortable in the presence of his fellow humans, especially the female ones. Apart from the skulls of dead fellwalkers on Knott in *The Northern Fells,* the people in the pictures are mostly himself—seen from behind. The one time he was comfortable with others was when telling them the best way up a hill.

But even on hills he wasn't altogether happy. Somewhere I've read that his feet were size eleven: however large or small, they tended to trip over the boulders. Harry Griffin has described him as no climber, noticeably clumsy and awkward even as a walker.

When things got steep Wainwright got nervous, and when things got rocky he broke into colourful and anxious prose. The trodden and popular Jack's Rake on Pavey Ark, now classed as a Grade 1 scramble, was in *The Central Fells* 'a series of convulsions unrelated to normal walking'. The short and slightly exposed summit rock of Helm Crag seems to have defeated him completely. At any rate, in that same book, a corner of a page was 'reserved for an announcement that the author had succeeded in surmounting the highest point'—but the volume went to press with the highest point still unsurmounted. It's possible that he achieved it at some date after 1958, but if so, no record remains. Thus Wainwright himself probably never completed the full list of 214 hills in his *Pictorial Guide*.

On the other hand, as someone whose spare-time occupation was being a municipal accountant in the borough treasurer's office in Kendal, he was determined not to short-change his public. This sense of duty and efficiency sent him into everywhere. And everywhere includes some pretty exciting places: bracken jungles, shifting screes and slimy corners—collectively they could be called Wainwright's Nasty Ways Up…

smillie

Helm Crag

A corner as slimy as any is the ten-foot chock-stone route up Loft Crag in Langdale (*The Central Fells* again). It's a route that diverts off the popular Dungeon Ghyll path either because its walkers weren't paying attention and accidentally took the climbers' path to Gimmer Crag, or because Gimmer is well worth getting a closer look at anyway. (Or for Reason One but then pretending Reason Two rather than admitting the mistake.)

Understandably unwilling to tackle the classic V Diffs and Severes without a rope, the route then takes to steep grass among rocky bits and finds itself channelled into a small blind gully. Wainwright scrambled up over the chockstone. This is awkward in October when covered in melting slush, so instead I took a crack in the gully wall thirty feet to the right. Either way, with bracken-scratched hands and with gravel rattling in the boots, he and I end up on grassy ledges high above Langdale: Wainwright fifty years in the past, me in what I consider to be the present day, both of us arriving suddenly and slightly short of breath at familiar Loft Crag from a quite unfamiliar direction.

And so, behind the tidy writing and meticulously laid-out pages, there does lurk a real adventurer. Many of these adventures are interesting but not actually enjoyable—take the Dove Crags route up Grasmoor, which is a lot of steep heathery pebbles and a very small amount of dirty rock.

On the other side of the same range, Tower Ridge on Eel Crag at the top of Coledale is a route where 'ladies in ankle-length skirts may find odd places a little troublesome'. The name given to it by Wainwright is definitely overstating the mark for anyone who knows the real Tower Ridge on Ben Nevis.

Pillar Rake on Mellbreak is an in-betweenie. The heather is horrid and very steep, but the rake itself is great: a grassy gangway that passes behind four little pinnacles, with damp crag above and nasty gullies below. Looking out past the pinnacles you see empty air, Crummock Water and Grasmoor. But with an hour of the very steep heather to get to it, and only twenty minutes of route when you've got there, Pillar Rake sees more sheep than people. The best idea may be to take a picnic up the north ridge and pop into Pillar Rake from the top—a cairn at grid reference NY147194 marks the place. Those who believe they've got to suffer to have fun will take Pillar Rake from the lakeside. I've done it, and I think it's a rake mistake.

Wainwright never pretends a place is nice when it actually isn't. Apart from his precision and his pictures, his great strength as a guidebook writer is his grumpiness—a trait he shared with the other notable guidebook writer, William Wordsworth. Wordsworth's *Guide to the Lakes* contains a superb twig-by-twig condemnation of the larch tree, extending over two full pages, as well as bad-tempered bits about modern nineteenth-century tourists and railway trains, and a real slagging-off for certain of the tarns. In the same vein, Wainwright waxes bolshily lyrical over the Pennine Way—and over the ravines between the ridges on Blencathra. So unattractive are these ravines, as described in *The Northern Fells*, that they actually sound rather fun.

My day of Blencathra Bad Ones started in Blease Gill, of which Wainwright wrote: 'Hard travelling over tough ground and wastes of scree make this no route for genteel walkers, but rough-necks will enjoy it.' Blease Gill turns out to be a way up Blencathra that is completely different from Sharp Edge, Hall's Fell, or the Glenderamackin. You start off not up the hill, but into it, on green stream-banks that lead under high heather. After hopping half-a-dozen times across the beck, you turn right into a scree-filled gully: 'The canyon is Wild West stuff—"gulch" might be a better word.' AW's favourite off-hill form of fun was going to see films about cowboys, so this is high praise indeed for Blease Gill. Above the gulch the slope opens into a scree fan, but you can avoid that on the right and arrive a small level place called Knott Halloo. And from there, one of Blencathra's less-trodden ridges leads sharply and suddenly to Gategill Fell Top. Blease Gill is a delightful way up Blencathra, a fell which already has so many delightful ways up. And truly, one's neck need not be all that rough.

I descended by Gate Gill: heather and stones, one of Wainwright's nasty ways that really is nasty.

And then I moved a few furlongs across the face to Doddick Gill. 'This is the roughest way of all. There is no comfort in it … For tough guys only … Not to be used for descent … A route to commend heartily to one's worst enemy.'

It may be that AW meant to add to the tribulations of his worst enemy by getting him lost; or else the sheep have been eating the scenery hereabouts. However, any slight thinness in his description scarcely matters. Of the hundred thousand who have bought *The Northern Fells*, and who have looked at the diagram of Doddick Gill, you have to wonder just how many have ever been up here. Even, conceivably, I may have been the first in the forty years since Wainwright wrote it.

After the initial wander in along the beck, the scramble 'using heather as handholds' is now a small path on the left, and this also avoids what sounds like wet feet 'along the slabby bed of the stream'. Above that, however, came a ravine several degrees more Wildly Western and gulchy than Blease Gill. A waterfall splashed in over the rim, then rode the wind uphill, to dampen my back during the next stages of the ascent. Wainwright didn't say on which side I was to escape to the 'bilberry slope', and anyway the sheep had eaten the bilberries, so I stayed in the ravine. There I found two little pitches of dubious rock with water running down them, so I got my wet feet after all, and a wet rest-of-me on top of the feet.

The ravine petered out in a face of grass and gravel, with crag shadow looming in the mist. I came across a water bottle, and a half-rotted woolly hat. I was reminded of the point beneath the North Ridge of Everest where climbers falling from above tend to fetch up: somewhere overhead was that nemesis of woolly hats, the breezy trade-route of Hall's Fell. And eventually I emerged on it just below its fine final scramble. Not all of AW's worst way had been nice—but, apart from a bit at the bottom, none at all of it had been boring.

Slightly shorter, slightly easier, but otherwise a whole lot better is the north ridge of Eagle Crag (*The*

smillie

Towards Knott from Castle Head

Central Fells). The whole point of Eagle Crag is the view of it you get from Stonethwaite. And straight up the front from Stonethwaite is the only way to walk it, for the good reason that, taken from the sides, Eagle Crag overhangs, and taken from the back, it doesn't actually exist—it's just a knoll at the corner of a moor.

Eagle Crag really ought to be the 'Langstrath Matterhorn'. As with the one at Zermatt, the fearsome appearance is achieved because the gentler ridge is pointing directly into the camera. And one suspects that Wainwright, like Whymper, has seen his hill from the side. Up he goes, anyway, on ledges zigzagging among rock bands.

At the crucial point a grassy gully provides the way through, after which Wainwright wanders off sideways to admire the overhang, does a sort of corkscrew over on the right, and hopes there are picnickers at the cairn waiting to be surprised as his flat cap pops up suddenly out of the abyss.

One or two of the Wainwright off-route routes are classics. The one I haven't tried yet is the South-West Arete of Skiddaw Little Man: 'First ascent, 4th September 1960 (First by A Wainwright, anyway!)' Still today it looks to be a route with more pinnacles than people, where 'inexperienced fellwalkers soon learn to distinguish, by trial and error, between bilberries and sheep-droppings, the former having decidedly the sweeter taste'. Yes, AW and WW are equally good at grumpiness, but AW scores higher on the sense-of-humour bit.

Nicest of all the Wainwright nasty ways up is the Grasmoor End Arete. Was it, too, unclimbed until the AW ascent? We shall never know, just as we shall never know whether the poet Coleridge was actually the first person to come down Broad Stand. That said, the End Arete is too steep and rocky to tempt any ordinary walker—and too heathery and broken for a prospective climber. What rock there is is the wrong sort: the despised Skiddaw slate. Someone may have been attracted up it under snow, on a day when the gullies of Great End were hidden under a blizzard. But it is just possible that Wainwright achieved a genuine first ascent.

What he certainly did achieve was the feel of a first ascent. It's not just our hats that are woolly: we hill humans are more like sheep than we care to admit. Venturing where none has been before is truly scary, while places that actually are scary but which have a few footprints are just fine. Up he goes, with only his eye to guide him, clinging to the heather stalks with a nasty drop below. Will he get out at the top? This isn't Central Buttress on Scafell, and yes, in all probability he will. There are still, incidentally, such authentic ascents to be had in busy Lakeland today. I found one in the summer of 2003 on the south ridge of Barf, where I had to balance the indignity of descent against loose turf, soggy rock, and the possibility of personal injury.

My choice, of course, was up: Barf is, after all, one of the Wainwright tops. Wainwright's own decision on Grasmoor End was easier. The start is on steep scree, with bilberry and crowberry and heather so you get a good gazetteer of your basic montane shrubs; AW also notes 'excellent specimens of prostrate juniper'. But once up that, Grasmoor End just gets nicer. The small ledges take you up to the base of the first tower, which you can bypass in a heathery groove on the left. Any actual rockwork is voluntary, although one little crest does offer some spectacular snapshots if your companion angles the camera to avoid the heather just below. Above the tower a ridgeline develops, and though the rock is now obligatory, it is very easy-angled or even horizontal. The situation is magnificent: if you wanted, you could drop your sandwich crusts straight into Crummock Water. Such behaviour would be sordid, and might compromise the healthy diet of the local ospreys. But even so, the top of the spur is a far better picnic spot than Grasmoor's summit cairn, which sits viewless at the centre of a stony plateau.

Grasmoor End Arete is not quite a Grade 1 scramble (the easiest grade). Rather, 'on the whole the climb is probably less difficult than the North Wall of the Eiger' (which had received its first British ascent by Bonington and Clough in 1962, just two years before Wainwright wrote those words). It may be technically straightforward, but it is still a genuine mountain route. A bad man is still a man: a poor poet is still a poet. And Wainwright, however big his feet, is still a real mountaineer. The essence of it, on the Eigerwand or on Grasmoor, is in the starting at the bottom and not quite knowing if you're going to get out at the top. Death is, of course, a lot less likely on Grasmoor: but it's still there as an intriguing possibility. And in the 1960s, on a weekday, on an unclimbed spur above Crummock, Wainwright's bones were going to get picked pretty clean before anybody disturbed the ravens.

For Lakeland rockclimbers today, the only chance of a new route is on some damp overhanging quarry down in the oakwoods. For scramblers, though, it is still feasible to get into awkward and irreversible situations in places not noted in either of Bryan Evans' two scrambling guides. And even for ordinary walkers there remain a few unpathed, unwritten fellsides where, like Wainwright on Grasmoor or on Eagle Crag, you can find a line with your eye and see if your feet can achieve it.

Ignorance leads to excitement. And so, on the Eskdale approach to Scafell Pike, on the Warnscale face of Haystacks, on some shattered side of Hindscarth, the true follower of AW is the one who doesn't buy his guidebook.

A tale of two trails
Along and across the Pennines

 With his Domesday Book of the Lakeland Fells duly done, if not dustjacketed, there might well have been a Gibbon-like moment as Wainwright laid down his pen in whatever passed for that famous summerhouse. But if there was, it did not last long. For, in his concluding notes to *The Western Fells,* he had already informed his readers that he was pledged to complete a Companion to the Pennine Way.

The book was to take the form of an annotated strip-map accompanied by illustrations, and the initial preparation was typically thorough. Even before *The Western Fells* had been finished, he had engaged four associates to assist in the preliminary survey: Mr Len Chadwick of Oldham, Mr Lawrence W Smith of Bradford, Mr Harry Appleyard of Wigton and Mr Cyril Moore of Morecambe. They were given their own patch, maps and precise instructions to check, from every source available, the exact location of the Official Footpath. Once confident that this had been done, they were to mark the route neatly in black waterproof Indian ink using Wainwright's tried and trusted formula to distinguish the nature of the land to be traversed. He also provided each with a cheque to cover expenses, with the instruction that if there was any surplus it should not be returned but spent 'in riotous living'. Their work was to be completed by Christmas 1965—the same date he was to give when signing off *The Western Fells*. He would walk the Way in the following two years; the book would be published in 1968. Job done.

It is clear that Wainwright particularly enjoyed planning the structure of the book. Unlike *A Pictorial Guide to the Lakeland Fells*, the seven volumes of which were a series of short stories about a variety of hills, this was to be a novel with a beginning, middle

and end and follow the traditional pattern of that other pilgrim's progress. The Celestial City was the Border Hotel at Kirk Yetholm and the description of his journey would warn against the many pitfalls and perils that might befall the unwary traveller:

Lothersdale is friendly, as few places on the Pennine Way are, and here for the first time since leaving Edale most walkers will feel a reluctance to proceed and a temptation to linger and enjoy the peaceful hospitality.

At this stage, however, he had not foreseen the extent of the Valleys of Humiliation or the Sloughs of Despond—nor the penance to be paid before a return to his Delectable Mountains.

He did, however, foresee one problem and this concerned the general layout. In Wainwright's view all maps should have north at the top and south at the bottom. As the book was in effect a map, albeit split into separate pages, then north should be at the beginning (or top) of the book and south at the end. However, as the official route progressed from Edale in the south to Kirk Yetholm in the north, Wainwright decided that his description had to start on the last page of the book, with the map and commentary steadily unleafing towards the first. This might seem, to the casual reader, that he was taking the concept of novelty a little too literally. But, as with most things he did, Wainwright was determined that the book should have an imprint of its own. Or, perhaps, he already had his eye on the Eastern market.

Much as Wainwright enjoyed the preparation, the actual journey was not a happy one. In the book's Introduction, no doubt out of a sense of obligation to his publishers, he describes the Way as a 'jolly good walk'; and, as he approved of the principles that lay behind Tom Stephenson's efforts to get the route officially recognised, he applauded the 'imaginative conception of a continuous way for travellers on foot across half of England'. In his Conclusion, however, there was a different tale: he was glad it was over, the 'floundering in glutinous peatbogs, the stumbling in soggy heather, the squelching in muddy fields', and he vowed that you would never see him anywhere near the place again. If the *Pictorial Guide* was a 'love letter', then the *Pennine Way Companion* was a tax return.

The question is why he found it so disappointing. It was not that he disliked walking in the Pennines. As a young man he had planned and completed his own Pennine Way from Settle to Hadrian's Wall and, on completion, he produced a draft manuscript entitled *Pennine Campaign*. He took enormous care with the project, compiling an accompanying 'Publisher's Booklet' which announced the arrival of a new literary talent and, in addition, a cod review praising its virtues. He was proud of his effort and hawked it around his friends and acquaintances in the hope, one assumes, that they might be on nodding terms with a publisher. But perhaps therein lies a clue to his later dissatisfaction. The current Pennine journey was not his creation and his commentary suggests that if he had been allowed his own Way, matters would have been rather different.

In the first place he felt that Stephenson's route wasn't a Pennine way at all. At least a fifth of it was in Northumberland after the Pennines had petered out. In Wainwright's view, a proper Pennine Way would begin in Dovedale and finish at Hadrian's Wall. The route should also stick to the watershed or at least include as much high land as possible, rather than meandering through farmyards and along canal towpaths. Another black mark against the Authorised Version, of which less than a quarter is over 1500 feet and considerably less than that if you lopped off the inDelectable Cheviot.

On top of this, Wainwright was unlucky with the weather during 1966 and 1967, and the struggle with soggy peat and sodden maps nearly made him give up on a number of occasions. Of course it is the measure of the man that he didn't. But was it really as bad as he made out? As any reader of Thomas Hardy will recall, the condition of the mind and the state of the weather can easily become intermingled—and at the time of writing, Wainwright's domestic life was in turmoil. He was separated from his first wife in increasingly acrimonious circumstances, and although he had found his 'Dream Girl', fantasised over in the original *Pennine Campaign*, he was far from convinced that all would turn out for the best. He was still married and feared either financial ruin or that a rival might step in before he could make an acceptable offer. Then there was his position as borough treasurer. Sexual liberation may well have arrived with the Beatles' first LP, but I doubt whether it would have yet swept through the ranks of the middle classes of Kendal.

It is very easy to make facts fit theories and indulge in fanciful connections between writer and text, but, in retrospect, we can see how his anguish seeped like the rain into his writing. We now know that the anonymous dedication to 'The one who helped most of all' was to his future wife Betty McNally, and that her favourite colour, turquoise, was chosen for the book's cover. But, even without hindsight, the text itself offers interesting if somewhat muted support to the idea that he was fed up with more than the elements. His assessment that seeking 'refuge under a lady's umbrella' was 'the crowning ignominy for a seasoned fellwalker' might well have had more than a literal meaning, and there are two illustrations that possibly reveal more than the obviously apparent.

The first, early in the Walk, is a picture of the Wain Stones on Bleaklow. These are two rocks worn by the weather to resemble a couple apparently about to kiss yet eternally separated. Beneath, Wainwright has written the legend: '(This is the only bit of sex in the book.)' You could assume that this is another piece of mock prudery meant to amuse his readers, but it may, on this occasion, have had an ironic subtext. As he plodded his way down to Crowden, he might well have been considering the coincidence of his name and the so-near-but-yet-so-far implications of the petrified lovers.

The second drawing comes much later in the journey. Illustrating his description of the Way as it follows the Tees is a picture of Low Force, one of the many waterfalls in the area. In the foreground, perched on a grassy mound, is a female hillwalker. This is unusual in itself, for Wainwright, as his advice on straddling barbed wire without irredeemable damage testifies, assumed that his readership was exclusively male. Although the pose guarantees anonymity, the general configuration conforms to photographs of Betty at the time. Moreover, the tone of the prose is considerably more upbeat than before, with terms such as 'delightful' and 'a charming stroll' replacing the previous 'wet and weary trudge'. His delight at reaching Middleton in Teesdale—'Chips, beer, ice-cream. Yippee!'—and his warnings to courting couples to beware of snakes in the long grass, suggest a very different state of mind from that which has gone before. Did he, perhaps, persuade Betty to accompany him on this easy section of the route? Well, something cheered him up, if only temporarily. The following day has the laconic comment: 'A less interesting interlude.' In the end, perhaps what was troubling him was not so much 'weather' as 'whether'.

If this line of reasoning seems rather too tenuous, it could call as witness that Wainwright was not above a bit of psychobabble when linking the lie of the land and that of the heart. He describes

Smillie
Dufton Pike

the Pennine Way as 'masculine', a hard taskmaster waiting for you to fail. On the other hand his next long-distance venture, *A Coast to Coast Walk across the North of England*, has 'feminine characteristics', tempting the walker, rewarding effort, massaging the ego. But whatever caused the despair of the Pennine Way, it is clear that during 1971 and 1972 there were two things that made him approach his trip from St Bees Head to Robin Hood's Bay with renewed confidence and optimism. First, he was master of his own destiny: the route would rely on his investigation and judgement. And now that he had remarried he could at last, if a little obliquely, introduce Betty to his readers: 'Everybody has a car nowadays, even me (and, in my case a good looking competent chauffeur to go with it).'

The Coast to Coast travelled through and linked together three National Parks, and Wainwright was confident that this would allow him to fulfil his initial criteria. These were: to avoid towns, keep to the high ground whenever he could, and give a wide berth to infuriated farmers and overfamiliar cows. Although he doesn't say so, he probably added a personal caveat—Avoid the Pennine Way, if humanly possible. With the exception of a deliberate visit to Richmond, he succeeded on all counts and must have been well satisfied with his research. Nor did the print layout cause any difficulty on this occasion. The route fell across the country and, as the prevailing weather suggested a west-to-east crossing, Wainwright's strip-maps would complement the text by entering on the left-hand margin and exiting on the right. In addition his experience of working on the *Pennine Way Companion* must have smoothed out most of the technical wrinkles.

There are, however, a number of additional factors

that make the Coast to Coast a more successful walk than the Pennine Way. Wainwright's route is more exploratory and takes the walker into less familiar territory. In the end, the Pennine Way is little more than a series of well-trodden excursions linked by narrow bands of boggy moorland and bullock-bedevilled field paths. The Coast to Coast is more elastic and allows diversions and alternatives to suit both the individual and the conditions. If the motive behind the creation of the Pennine Way was political, then that behind the Coast to Coast was aesthetic.

It also has better shape. Whereas the Pennine Way could have started and finished in a variety of places, the chosen Coast to Coast termini, unless you can walk on water, are distinct. Unlike the Pennine Way, with its unavoidable twenty-nine mile trudge to hammer the final northern nails into the coffin, Wainwright's Coast to Coast route can be broken into convenient lengths with adequate B&B accommodation. (For those who require greater stimulation than fresh air and fine views, the Campaign for Real Ale produces a useful list of hostelries who offer an extra B.)

And then there is the endgame. The last stretch to Kirk Yetholm had been punctuated with exhortations such as 'Don't give in. The agony will soon he over', and a countdown of the inclines to climb and the yards to go before the destination—'At last!'— hoved into view. The entrance to Robin Hood's Bay, in contrast, is deliberately delayed. The reader is taken on an excursion to follow the 'royal road' of the coastpath and any attempt to take a short cut is met with the clear instruction to 'carry on down the lane and don't argue'. At the Border Hotel, Wainwright, almost by way of apology, offers to buy any comple-tionist a free drink. Not so at the Bay, where if you order a pint there is to be no misunderstanding: 'It's no use saying "charge it to Wainwright" as you did at Kirk Yetholm. No, sonny, that game won't work here. Pay for your own.' I suspect he felt that, on this occa-sion, it was he rather than the reader who was owed a reward. At the end he summed up the two experi-ences thus: 'I finished the Pennine Way with relief, the Coast to Coast with regret.'

But what really gave the second enterprise its energy and drive was that he could return afresh to his beloved Lake District. Although he must have been tempted to allow the fells the honour of welcoming the triumphant arrival, he knew he could plan a route that would give such a kick-start that it would motivate the rest of the journey. He also knew, all too well, how a bad beginning can destroy morale—a good soaking on the North York Moors might have had the same effect as a similar drowning on Bleaklow or Black Hill. And there is no doubt that he was up for it. Throughout this opening Lakeland section there is a continuous presence of an enthusiastic, avuncular figure taking his favourite nephews on a guided tour of a secret garden.

As with the best of uncles, he offers encouragement and caution in appropriate measure. If you choose the upland route of his 'High Stile Alternative', you can class yourself as one of nature's 'supermen'; but if the weather closes in over the Grisedale Pass, you are to 'contemplate neither' of the possible expeditions to Helvellyn or St Sunday Crag and go immediately into the valley (do not pass Go, do not collect £200). But whatever the weather, he will point out the sights, be they stone circles, an abundance of bog asphodel or, after you have passed the point of doing any possible harm, the haunt of golden eagles.

One of the best parts of this section occurs when he bounds into Borrowdale. Not only is the dale 'the fairest of valleys', strewn with hanging gardens of rowan or birch and studded with cliffs and whitewashed cottages, but it is also the gateway to a fine piece of cross-country walking. The route from Seatoller to Haweswater runs against the grain and a switchback of ranges have to be crossed rather than valleys followed. Wainwright's elegant route makes the best of the ground and if you walk it alone you can catch the reverberation of ancient footfalls that must have travelled from thwaite to thwaite in this long-inhabited region. Of course, you are let off the leash from time to time (weather permitting) to scale the heights, whereupon inclusive panoramic diagrams

Causey Pike, Barrow & Grisedale Pike from Keswick landings   Smillie

are duly dispensed. Such is Wainwright's confidence in a job well done that he can teasingly tempt his reader to abandon the Coast to Coast and spend the rest of the holiday in Lakeland. Of course, he is quick to point out that he was only joking and you'll jolly well have to go on and finish it or never look him in the eye again.

He knew the Lakes would be a hard act to follow, but was determined to give it his best shot. The springy turf of Westmorland limestone was praised; the route from Kirkby Stephen to Keld escaped with only a hundred yards of Pennine Way contagion; the history of lead mining in Swaledale is given the full treatment—if you didn't know what a 'hush' was before, you do now; and the stretch from Reeth to Richmond receives more compliments that the sweet lass of her eponymous Hill. The dull twenty miles of the Vale of Mowbray are skipped over expeditiously and the walker is advised to do the same.

In the final section over the North York Moors, Wainwright exudes bonhomie. He, almost, ignores the opportunity to complain about damage done to the landscape by the gliding fraternity. He praises the variety of scene ranging from prehistoric relics to steam locomotives. And, when he reaches a second set of Wainstones, his description suggests Yorkshire pleasure rather than Derbyshire pain. At the last, he leads his entourage into Robin Hood's Bay with the usual promises of untold opportunities for self-indulgence.

During the walk Wainwright must have spent some time mulling over the merits or otherwise of the official Long Distance Footpath, for he decides in the end that the whole idea is a bad thing. His reasons are *(a)* it attracts the wrong sort of people; *(b)* that driving hordes of walkers along a narrow strip of land will quickly destroy it and/or become a nuisance to those who live and work there; and *(c)* it discourages personal initiative. (Interestingly enough the same three objections could be levelled against his *Pictorial Guide to the Lakeland Fells*, but Wainwright rarely allows logic to interfere with prejudice.) He exempts his own Long Distance Footpath from similar criticism on the grounds that it is more an example than a route. He urges his readers to discover their own variations or, better still, to get out their maps and plan a way of their own. If these suggestions have opened the eyes of his disciples to the possibility of avoiding the badly beaten-up path, then he will have done a service to them as well as the countryside at large.

That is not to say that he didn't fancy himself as the Pied Piper. The book's dedication (to the second person to walk from St Bees Head to Robin Hood's Bay) indicates a hope that others will follow in his footsteps. Yet I am sure that he could never have imagined it serving as inspiration to an American opera singer. In January 2004, David Pisaro planned a rendering of Schubert's song cycle *Winterreise*. In a Stanislavski moment he decided not only to complete the Coast to Coast but also to stage performances at his various stopping points. His venues included churches, bookshops and, on one occasion, a farmhouse parlour. (The accompanying piano travelled by road rather than rucksack but even its journey had one or two twists and turns of its own.) Pisaro's explanation was that, as the protagonist was a lovesick wanderer travelling on foot through the depths of winter, he could think of no better way of getting into character than plodding across the North of England in the bitter cold and wet.

Wainwright, I feel, would have directed him not to St Bees Head but the Nag's Head at Edale.

Interlude
A few thoughts on fellbagging

Wainwright has become half-man, half-list. The flat-capped fellwanderer might have set out to write a series of guidebooks, but in the subsequent decades his readers have, in considerable numbers, turned the *Pictorial Guide* into a tick-list of baggable hills. This was surely inevitable, whether or not to everyone's liking, since to visit all of Wainwright's hills is to make a *de facto* completion of his 'list'. Hence the concept of 'Wainwrights': 214 summits in all, this being the total of individual fell-chapters in the seven books (35, 36, 27, 30, 24, 29 and 33 fells respectively). Some walkers tack on the 102 bumps and lumps contained within the later *Outlying Fells*, but the most commonly accepted definition of having 'done the Wainwrights' involves having paid a visit to each of 214 felltops.

Despite what the list-detractors might say, there is nothing inherently wrong or unhealthy in this. The anti-argument usually goes thus: to categorise hills is to diminish them, and since when have the inscrutable, timeless, majestic (add your own overblown adjective here) hills ever had anything to do with the reductive, anal-retentive, anorakish world of lists and wilful documentation? But that's surely unfair—and it's worth noting that this kind of criticism only ever seems to flow one way. It's a rare day indeed when a list-user is to be heard slagging a 'real' hill-lover for their non-use of lists.

The gradual evolution of Wainwright's seven main books into a formal structure for exercise and enjoyment is surely a good thing, if only at the axiomatic level that it encourages more people to find out what

smillie

Dale Head - looking to Skiddaw

all the fuss is about with the fells. A list, any list, prompts walkers into going out regularly on all kinds of terrain and in all weathers, bolstering their navigational skills and ensuring that, from time to time, they're *in situ* high on a ridge for that great moment when a poor day starts to improve into cloud-shredding clarity, a joy that the fair-weather walker will never know.

Having a specified set of target summits also allows for odd-but-interesting concoctions of routes to be devised, outings where unlikely combinations of hills are strung together. The Lakeland fells, with their crammed-together, almost claustrophobic feel, are ideal for this kind of mix'n'match day—a big fell here, a little fell there—and many walkers must surely have returned home of an evening feeling satisfied (if not sated) with the day's varied bag of summits. There is even scope for using the established structure of Wainwright's books for formal bagging games: try, for instance, to take in summits from as many of the seven books as possible in a single day's on-foot outing. Easy enough, relatively speaking, if the books concerned are the Southern, Central and Western volumes; less easy (but quite possibly more fun) if trying to combine North Western with Far Eastern.

꙳ ꙳ ꙳

Alan Castle of the Long Distance Walkers' Association maintains a list of those people known to have been round all 214 Wainwright summits. Updated versions of this people-list are published each year in the LDWA magazine *Strider*, and by the end of 2003 the number of known Wainwright 'completions' had reached 331. The first recorded finish is that of Alan Barber on 30 April 1966, just four months after Wainwright had signed off Book Seven, and a considerable number of walkers have been round more than once. (The record for this belongs to Stephen Moore, who at the last count had completed fifteen full rounds, including four during 2003. That's keen.)

Then there are the unlisted completions: people who have climbed all 214 fells but who remain unrecorded either because they don't want to be in (through modesty, disapproval or simple can't-be-bothered-ness) or because they don't know that such a list exists. As to how many 'refusniks' there are, it's anyone's guess—Castle admits to not really having 'the faintest idea'. He does, however, offer an estimate that the real figure could be 30–50 percent higher than the recorded one—and, from what is known of other hill categories, this seems reasonable. So it's fairly safe to say that, at the time of writing, at least 400 people, quite possibly 500-plus, have followed in Wainwright's bootsteps and stood on all 214 of 'his' summits.

Or have they? This might seem a strange, even absurd question, but bear with me. The most celebrated hill list is that compiled in 1891 by Hugh Munro, who detailed 283 Scottish 3000ft summits along with a further 255 subsidiary tops. Revisions have come and gone, and the current figure is 284 main summits (which have become known simply as Munros) and 227 Tops. (Strictly speaking, all 511 summits count as Tops, but this isn't the place to go into such subtleties.) The main difference, in terms of compilation, is that Munro deliberately set out to list a category of hills, whereas Wainwright set out to produce guidebooks which later evolved, for many walkers, into a tick-list. The difference is evident in the periodic publication, usually furiously debated, of revisions to the Munros, be they 'objective' revisions caused by remapping, such that a hill previously thought to be under 3000ft turns out to be above that mark (or *vice versa*), or 'subjective' revisions where the editor of the day decides that a particular summit is or isn't separate enough from its neighbour, and so its status is changed. This latter type of revision prompts particular debate, and some doubt its merit. Few, however, would quibble with the first type of change, and were a completely new Scottish 3000ft hill to be discovered—on a Brigadoon-meets-Atlantis island in the Minch, for example—there would be a strong consensus for its inclusion in the list of Munros. This, ultimately, is because Munro himself would have wanted it that way. He saw his list as an attempt to document something that had previously been a matter of conjecture and estimation, and he was working on the first revision (eventually published in 1921) when he died in 1919.

Compare this with the Wainwrights. Because Wainwright was producing guidebooks and not lists, he was able, perfectly reasonably, to choose what to include. There were no rules beyond those that he himself invented, and he broke one of these (that fells should be 1000ft or more) when *The North Western Fells* included Castle Crag, a mere 985ft. But as with the idiosyncratic southern boundary to the overall *Pictorial Guide* area[1], this was OK: it was Wainwright's choice, so he could do what the heck he liked.[2]

What this means in terms of revisions to the list

Lingmell

of Wainwrights is simple: there will never be any. Even 'objective' changes are inadmissible, so were a major peak to suddenly materialise (say an earthquake caused a chunk of Pillar to sheer off and leave a new free-standing fell above Ennerdale, a kind of super-Steeple), then it still couldn't qualify as a Wainwright. The only way that such a canonical change could have happened was if Wainwright himself had suggested it or agreed to it, but now that option has gone for ever. Hence the occasional debates about the make-up of the list are redundant. Those fells that are scarcely separate at all (most notably the nigh-on summitless Mungrisdale Common) will always be in the list. Equally, those missing fells that merit a chapter of their own remain forever locked out. So it's hard luck (but quieter slopes) for Darling Fell, or Knock Murton, or—most contentious of all—the 3000ft summits of Ill Crag and Broad Crag, both of which would easily qualify as Munro Tops were they located north of the border. These, and others like them, only appear within other chapters (on, respectively, Low Fell, Blake Fell and, for the latter pair, Scafell Pike). Fine fells though they are, they're never going to acquire the status of the 214, because the books comprise a closed system, and that's that.

Now, back to the question of whether people have actually ticked off their Wainwrights. Just as the set of 214 fells is unalterable, so the 214 points to which Wainwright allocated his 'summit' label is likewise fixed. This might seem an ultra-pedantic truism, but it matters. There are instances of Wainwright opting for a summit which is now known—and perhaps was known at the time—to be not the strict highpoint of the fell. Two examples feature in *The Southern Fells*: Illgill Head and Whin Rigg. These are the main bumps on the plateau above the Wastwater Screes, and in each instance Wainwright decrees that 'The Summit' is at the cliff-edge, whereas modern maps show that both actual summits lie 'inland' a bit. So where does that leave a would-be Wainwright-bagger who visits the true 1998ft point on Illgill Head but not Wainwright's 1983ft summit at the edge? Such a person has undoubtedly reached the top of the fell, but has he or she ticked the Wainwright?

Even more awkward (and amusing) is the case of Helm Crag, the awkward rocky top of which Wainwright never reached, having been 'defeated by a lack of resolution'. Does this mean that Wainwright failed to complete a round of Wainwrights, just as Munro failed to complete a round of Munros?[3] Some would say yes, Wainwright only managed 213—but this is absurd given the particular subjectivity of the list. Clearly Wainwright reached his own requisite point on each fell, including Helm Crag, and so Alan Barber should be relegated to second place in the list of Wainwrightists, behind the great man himself. And as with the Illgill Head example, it could even be argued that touching the top of Helm Crag, and hence not 'failing' on it as did Wainwright, ought not to count in Wainwrightean terms. Fellgoing is neither simple nor straightforward, and oft-times there is something out-

and-out perverse about it. So there is an aptness in the notion that failing to fully climb a fell might merit a tick, whereas achieving the standard modern-world success of actually getting up it could fail to provide the collateral mark in the book.

A further refinement to this theory[4] is to argue that the requirement to complete a round of Wainwrights ought not to be just to reach the top of each fell (whether that be the true top or the Wainwright top). Rather, because the list is inextricable from the guidebooks, each of the *routes* so lovingly described by Wainwright should be trodden, whether on ascent or descent. This is easy on, say, Rannerdale Knotts, where just two routes are suggested: these could be combined in a round, and an unequivocal tick could then be inserted into the list. Less easy on Blencathra, the fell to which Wainwright devoted the most pages (thirty-six), where twelve ascent routes are given along with two connecting ridge-routes. Here a minimum of seven visits must be made before the fell can be considered well and truly Wainwrighted.

There are, ultimately, no real rules about all this, but the argument that routes should be walked rather than simple summits claimed is a healthy one, in that it treats the hill with respect, deals with it in a complete sense rather than just focusing on the summit cherry on top of the overall fell-cake (and often—at risk of stretching the metaphor—it is a massively complex cake; it's absurd to regard the enthrallingly complicated Coniston Old Man, for example, as just a summit to be visited).

This kind of repeat-visit approach has the merit of using the simplicity of the list-structure as a means to enjoy the inscrutable, timeless, majestic beauty of the fells. It's joined-up rather than dumbed-down, holistic rather than hastily minimal. It also seems entirely fair and reasonable, as fellgoing is surely about increasing knowledge and broadening experience. And most important of all, Wainwright, never one to shy away from revisiting a fell, would surely have approved.

Notes

1 See the introduction for more on this.

2 One of the things that makes the *Pictorial Guide* feel so true to Lakeland is Wainwright's depiction of hills of pretty much all heights. Lakeland contains such a clutter of hills, large and small, crammed into a small space, that it has a distinctively different feel to all other hill areas in the UK. Lochaber and the Cairngorms, for instance, are dominated by high ridges and plateaux—not much Catbells-sized stuff there—and whereas the wonderland of Assynt and Coigach does have plenty of relatively small hills, they are spaced much more widely than is the case in Borrowdale or up Tilberthwaite.

3 For a mishmash of reasons Munro never reached three of his Tops: Carn an Fhidhleir, Carn Cloich-mhuilinn and the Inaccessible Pinnacle. Only the first two were regarded as main summits, or Munros, at the time. Curiously, the Inaccessible Pinnacle was listed as a Top of Sgurr Dearg, even though the latter is plainly lower.

4 For more on this see Ann Bowker's piece later in this book.

The Book of Fells
Wainwright's graphic monument[1]

 Alfred Wainwright's achievement in producing his seven guides to the Lakes between 1952 and 1965 was a triumph of disciplined draughtsmanship. Each guide, in its original published form, was drawn from beginning to end, and demonstrated accomplished mastery of justified hand-lettering, drawing by line alone of maps, elevated views, outline views, graphs and other figures, and of mountain landscapes which combined accuracy with beauty. Moreover, he achieved a pleasing integration of all of these elements on the page. Each guide has around 300 pages, and while the introductory notes on Classification and Definition, and the Notes on the Illustrations are repeated from guide to guide, he must have drawn about 2000 such pages—on average, a new page every two days. Since he didn't draw on his weekend excursions to the mountains, and was still in full-time employment, it's

not hard to figure out how he spent his evenings.

This remarkable achievement would have been a *tour de force* even for a professional graphic artist trained in landscape work, map-drawing, etc. But Wainwright had no art training. Certainly he drew from an early age, and kept on drawing for his own amusement until he began his guidebook-drawing at the age of forty-five, but his reticent autobiographies[2] give no indication that he had drawn mountains beforehand. Yet the drawings in Book One are just as accurate, lively and effective as those in Book Seven—almost no graphic development is apparent, except for the gradual elimination of drawn skies.[3] He therefore invented himself as a master of all forms of pure line drawing in the space of a very few years, and at the same time rediscovered the perfect method of book publishing used in the mediaeval scriptoria of monasteries and palaces before the invention of the printing press—the copied illuminated manuscript.[4]

His methods are described here and there in the various autobiographical fragments, and some may be inferred from the books. He used pens that produced ink lines of constant width, in a range of sizes, but by and large stuck to one width of line when drawing landscapes. It might be guessed that the separate elements of each page were drawn on different papers, then cut and arranged to make a page of some convenient size larger than the intended publication size. However, the manuscript pages I have seen were all drawn on one piece of paper at the intended publication size. If an error was made (and these appear to have been very few) opaque white was used for correction, and sometimes a small piece was corrected by pasting on a drawn fragment.[5] Apparently, he used a magnifier and a strong light while drawing.[6] He took photographs of every landscape subject, and interpreted these in pure line. In *Fellwanderer*, there are a number of the photographs used, and in *Memoirs of a Fellwanderer* his photographs are often paired with matching drawings. It may be seen that these are reproduced faithfully, even the temporary features of light and shade. He 'confesses' to this method in *Fellwanderer* (text page 6), making it clear that he had neither time enough to draw on the spot, nor energy enough to carry stool, easel, etc, up hills, and disparaging himself (tongue firmly in cheek) as a 'cheat', 'cheapjack' and 'fraud'. He notes there that the camera lens 'tends to depress verticals and extend distances' and that these faults had to be corrected when drawing at home. But despite these remarks about the imperfections of the camera,[7] he doesn't seem to have made many such corrections, and so the drawings are sufficiently close to the photographs for us to wonder whether he may have used some method of projection. I doubt very much whether he had the means, inclination or time to do this: it is much more likely that he simply pinned or propped up the photograph above his drawing.

In English drawing, signs of particular attention to mountain form appeared in the eighteenth century in association with the literary/artistic movement known as The Picturesque. The well-known drawings of Francis Towne's Lakeland tour of 1786 provide excellent examples of a method often employed.[8] The outline of the mountains and occluding boundaries (edges of ridges, gullies, boulders, men or animals, trees, etc, which overlap hidden parts of the mountain) inside the outline, were rendered in ink line. Light and shade (tone) was added using watercolour washes. Since the outline is also an occluding boundary (hiding the other side of the mountain, or the sky), line is used in such drawings according to a strict principle: where there are no occluding boundaries, there are no lines. Moreover, if the artist faces a roughly conical mountain, there will be many occluding boundaries to the left and to the right, but few in the central projection of the mountain, so by and large the drawn lines will have the same degree and direction of slope as the feature drawn. So such occluding-boundary drawings portray the structure of a mountain very well, even if it is conceded (as it was in the mid-nineteenth century if not earlier) that there are no such lines in nature, only boundaries between foreground and background regions.

However, two problems with such an approach to drawing mountains (or indeed any smooth object such as a human or animal figure) arise immediately if the artist is restricted to the use of line. First, if there is a part of the mountain directly opposite the viewpoint, and therefore showing very few occluding contours, how is its structure to be drawn? Second, if it is desired to add tone, how is this to be done? The addition of tone is important, because it adds information about the structure of the mountain—more light falls on flat areas, and less light on steep areas.

In the eighteenth and nineteenth centuries, when such drawings were published, the printer would substitute line-shading for the tone supplied by ink or watercolour wash. These added lines were engraved or etched on the plate, or cut in wood. Truly tonal methods were also available to late eighteenth century printmakers—aquatint; and, by the mid-nineteenth century, lithography. However, these were expensive and tricky processes, and the bulk of nineteenth century illustration was achieved by line engraving.[9]

Draughtsmen and printmakers have always learned from each other, and many draughtsmen were printmakers too, so it is no surprise that the rendering of tone by line in a drawing is also commonplace. This practice is particularly evident in figure drawings, perhaps, but the same principles are applied in mountain drawing. Line tone may be added in two main ways, First, lines may be added parallel to the occluding boundaries on one side, so that the line marking the boundary becomes instead the edge of a dark area: this type of shading may be called vector shading, since as noted above such lines represent the steepness and direction of slopes quite accurately. Second, lines may be added that follow the principal curvature of the object—these have the dual effect of showing the curvature, and adding tone. In figure drawing, this latter sort of line shading is known

This drawing by Rowbotham sticks to vector shading for the mountains, avoiding conflict with the horizontal lines of sky and water. (Thomas Leeson Rowbotham: Fig 24 of The Art of Sketching from Nature, *Winsor & Newton, c 1870.)*

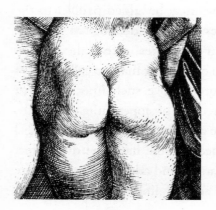

The use of both vector and bracelet shading gives this Dürer bottom power and solidity. (Albrecht Dürer: Die Vier Hexen, *detail, copper line engraving.)*

as bracelet shading. Lines that follow the principal curvature of a mountain are well-known to us from the study of maps—we call them contours, so I will refer to this type of line shading as contour shading. Obviously, contour shading will have exactly the same effect as on a map, together with the bonus of tonal effect: lines close together indicate steep areas and simulate dark tone, and widely-spaced lines indicate gentle slopes and simulate light tone. If both types of line shading are used in a drawing, cross-hatching of the disciplined sort familiar to us today from wire-frame models results.[10]

Whereas vector shading is to some degree natural, in that the occluding boundaries from which it derives its direction are real, contour shading is in general entirely conventional. Occasionally, drawn contours will correspond to some mountain feature—for example, 'lines' of stratification in limestone or sandstone hills, sheep-tracks, solifluction lobes, etc.

Once these preliminary observations and distinctions have been made, Wainwright's approach to drawing becomes evident. To an occluding-boundary drawing of the mountain he added both sorts of structural line

Mrs Almond's drawing of Suilven uses vector shading for the mountain's plinth and for Canisp, but contour shading dominates. The sky is sensibly left blank and water only indicated with broken lines. (Eleanora F Tristram (Mrs Hely H Almond): SMC Journal *IV, p 26, 1896.)*

tone, vector and contour shading. In the parts of the mountain receding from the viewpoint to left or right, vector shading tends to dominate; in the parts of the mountain opposite the viewpoint, contour shading tends to dominate. In addition, Wainwright's contour shading is usually a broken contour, with the breaks aligned to produce white 'lines' vertical on the page corresponding to features such as runs of scree, streams, etc. An excellent example of this is the drawing of Stac Polly on page 157 of *Memoirs…* The paired photograph allows us to see that an awkward inversion of tone is often involved, as here.

However, Wainwright's control and use of these two types of shading was absolute. He was capable of dispensing with either. For example, his drawing of Grasmoor from Mellbreak (page 182, *Memoirs...*) uses only vector shading for the mass of the mountain even though it sits directly opposite the viewpoint. Here he softens the effect of steepness by the use of broken or dotted vectors. He switches to contour shading at the base of the mountain. The transition is a touch abrupt, and perhaps the mountain appears a little too steep, but these are minor faults in a masterly drawing.[11] The Wastwater Screes (page 112, *Memoirs...*) are also directly opposite, and contour shading is employed only for a few grassy areas of the craggy face.[12]

On the other hand, many drawings, particularly in the later books, employ heavy use of contour shading, with vector shading used only for craggy areas, if at all. Yewbarrow 9, the last full-page drawing in the last book, is a case in point. In Book Six, Barrow 1 and Catbells 1 are pure contour-shaded drawings (there is some vector shading in the foreground of Barrow 1).

Most of the drawings in the seven books, however, follow the broad principles of line shading described above. What is constant and consistent in Wainwright's drawings, then, is his use of structural line shading—shading that reflects and reveals the steepness and direction of mountain slopes, whether by means of the vector principle, or the contour principle.

In his strict adherence to structural shading, he differs from others who have drawn mountains by means of line alone. It is much more common in such drawings to see tone added by arbitrary line shading, usually the default north-east to south-west diagonal shading favoured by right-handed drawers. Such shading, of course, corresponds to no feature of the mountain and adds nothing to the drawing except variation in tone. The drawings of Ellis Carr which illustrate Haskett Smith's *Climbing in the British Isles* are usually of this sort.[13] There are some exceptions: for example, 'Llyn Idwal' (*Wales*, page 42), 'Snowdon from Glaslyn' (*Wales*, page 70), and 'Snowdon from the South, with Lliwedd on the left' (*Wales*, page 74) use only structural shading. These are excellent and effective drawings and may be contrasted with the feeble Crib Goch drawings (*Wales*, pages 62 and 65) in which arbitrary diagonal shading is used. There are several drawings in the *England* guide where a comparison may be made between Carr and Wain-

Carr's drawing of Pavey Ark adds only arbitrary diagonal shading to the crag's outline. Compare with Pavey Ark 10 in Book Three. (W Haskett Smith: Climbing in the British Isles: England, *Longmans, 1894.)*

wright, to Wainwright's advantage. Napes Needle (*England*, page 94) is drawn from exactly the same viewpoint as the drawing in *Memoirs…*, page 198: Wainwright's painstaking structural approach (mostly vector shading) makes the blocks of which the Needle is composed seem massive, substantial and precisely shaped, whereas in Carr's drawing (arbitrary diagonal shading) the Needle appears to have been rather clumsily faced with irregular stone slabs. I could find no reference to Carr's drawings in Wainwright's writings. It would be interesting to know whether he studied his work. Certainly, the best of Carr is very similar to his own manner of drawing.

If there is any weakness in Wainwright's drawings, it is in his drawing of skies and of still water. As noted earlier, he gave up attempting to draw skies, having experimented with a range of methods. The three skies in Book Seven are all added to mountains which are vector-shaded: horizontal shading is used for the clear areas of sky, with implied clouds elsewhere, except for Fellbarrow 1 in which the clouds are outlined. There is an awkward collision of horizontal sky-shading and mountain vector-shading in Fellbarrow 1 on the right.

As for water, even in Book One he experimented with different methods. Birkhouse Moor 1 uses vague reflection for Lanty's Tarn. Other drawings in Book One omit reflections entirely and use horizontal shading as an indication of tone, with light areas of water left white, or—as in Glenridding Dodd 1—horizontal tone with some added reflection (cross-hatched). Without changing the width of line, or adopting some other convention to mark the distinction between land and water, these approaches are problematic, particularly when contour shading has been used for the lower parts of the mountain. Perhaps leaving water white, with the odd symbolic horizontal line, might have been a better method. Book Seven shows the same sort of range of methods, with the addition of precise reflection (eg Great Gable 1, very unconvincing). Flat valley bottoms, patterned with fields, present similar problems to standing water, and it cannot be said that he dealt with these very effectively either.

But we mountaineers are not aviators or meteorologists, nor are we sailors or farmers. We are interested in what intervenes between the valley bottoms and skies, and if what we desire is a mountain drawing that reveals the shape and detail of a mountain in every detail, and shows its beauty clearly, then there is no one who has done that more effectively than Alfred Wainwright.

Notes

1   I am grateful to Sue Beach, John Mitchell and Craig Smillie for advice regarding Wainwright's drawing methods. It should be made clear that this survey of Wainwright's work in the seven guides is based only on the published guides, and publications about them. I have had only very limited opportunity to study his manuscript pages. Obviously, a definitive assessment of his work and methods of working would require detailed study of the original works.

2   Each guide has a tailpiece, with some biographical content. In addition there are *Fellwanderer*, Westmorland Gazette, 1966; *Ex-Fellwanderer*, Westmorland Gazette, 1987; and *Memoirs of a Fellwanderer*, Michael Joseph, 1993, a posthumous compendium of the first two works.

3   The number of drawings with skies declines fairly regularly from forty-six in Book One to three in Book Seven (Fellbarrow 1, Grike 1 and Pillar 1).

4   Copied by machines, of course, rather than monks, but copied, not printed.

5   Several manuscript pages were displayed at the Wainwright Exhibition, 1 May to 31 August 2004, in the Kendal Museum.

6   The method used to print Wainwright's pages is not described anywhere, so far as I know. The page blocks used by the *Westmorland Gazette* for early editions were relief blocks. I presume that a contact print on high contrast film was first made from Wainwright's page, and this then was used in a photochemical process to etch out the white areas from the metal plate, leaving the lines in relief. I enquired at the *Westmorland Gazette*, but 40-odd years have been sufficient to erase any record or recollection of the actual process used.

7   Wainwright's camera was included in the Wainwright Exhibition referred to in note 5. Whether it was the camera used for the seven books I don't know, but it seems likely. It is a 1950s Russian Lubitel-2, made by LOMO, the Leningrad Optical and Mechanical Union (*Leningradskoye Optiko-Mekhanicheskoye Obyedineniye*). The camera is a twin-lens reflex model using roll-film, and taking twelve 6cm x 6cm exposures per film. It was a cheap mass-produced copy of the Voigtlander Brilliant camera, and capable of excellent work.

8 For examples, see Timothy Wilcox, *Francis Towne*, Tate Gallery Publishing, 1997.

9 Skilful engravers were capable of very closely-spaced ultra-fine parallel lines made with a needle point. When printed, such lines are no longer discernible. Excellent examples of true tone achieved by means of fine lines may be seen, for example, in early editions of Part V 'Of Mountain Beauty' of John Ruskin's *Modern Painters*.

10 In thinking about how to describe different approaches to line drawing, I found the discussions in John Willats' *Art and Representation* (Princeton University Press, 1997) helpful. My terminology is slightly different from Willats'.

11 In Grasmoor 1 (Book Six) the viewpoint is slightly different (further north and lower), the transition from vector to contour shading occurs higher on the mountain, and patches of contour shading are added to produce cross-hatched areas corresponding to small areas of crag high on the mountain.

12 In Whin Rigg 9/10 (Book Four) the Screes are drawn from a similar viewpoint. Here contour shading is used much more liberally in all parts of the drawing except for the bottom left area where broken vectors lead down to an area in which no shading is used: instead, thousands of tiny boulders are drawn.

13 Volume 1 of Smith's guide deals with England, Volume 2 with Wales.

What Alfred did next
Follow-ups, spin-offs and oddities

 In a few years' time, the seventh and (possibly) final Harry Potter tome will thud on to the nation's bookshelves. And so, as J K Rowling's demanding but lucrative project draws to a close, she will arrive at a Wainwright Moment. At the end of 1965, the fabled fellwanderer had faced the same What next? predicament as will the considerably more petite children's author. Wainwright's seven-book series, the *Pictorial Guide to the Lakeland Fells*, was complete, and the publishing industry being what it was (and is), he had to come up with something new. The reading public, so he was told, demanded it.

Wainwright's survey of the fells was many things: a passionate project and a publishing phenomenon for starters. But how do you follow an exercise that has consumed thirteen years of your life? Does Wainwright's experience provide any pointers for

Rowling? Well, if it does, she certainly needn't worry about writer's block. In the years after the completion of the Seven, Wainwright's publishing output became almost mind-bogglingly copious. I wonder if Rowling will manage to publish fifty books post-Potter?

Wainwright's first post-Seven work was *Fellwanderer*, a book which had some elements of shock value: there were pages and pages of photographs, it came in a larger and somewhat awkward-on-the-shelves landscape format and, while Wainwright's unmistakable pen-and-ink drawings played a large part in the rest of the book, the text was actually set in printer's type. So in many ways *Fellwanderer* was a departure from the Seven—yet it only made sense in connection with the series. It explained some of Wainwright's reasons for having undertaken the project, recounted a very few of his experiences in having carried it out and, most enjoyably, contained some reflections on fell-walking and the hills in general.

At that time, 1966, Wainwright was still a rather mysterious figure. Users of the Seven were desperate to find out more, and *Fellwanderer* was ostensibly designed to tell them more: it was, after all, subtitled *The Story Behind the Guidebooks*. Yet Wainwright the man remained private, even if a photograph of him, sketching away on the fells, was now in a published book. (*Fellwanderer* also included a gratuitous vintage snap of Wainwright the infant.) He still clung to the anonymity of a nameless initial—just as Joanne Kathleen hid behind the inscrutable J K—and he was only frank enough to tell his readers that his Christian name wasn't Aloysius. Nevertheless, there is much in *Fellwanderer* that is amusing and wry and insightful and moving. It's here, for example, that he announced his wish for his mortal remains to be scattered on Haystacks, little knowing that he still had twenty-five years and a small shedload of books to get through first.

So, by the end of 1966, the Seven had been completed and, in *Fellwanderer*, partly explained and justified. Was it, in the dread Blairite language of our own age, time to 'draw a line' and 'move on'? Within the massive explosion of Wainwrightean output in the late sixties and early seventies, there were several works that could be seen as continuations or extensions of the original project—albeit remaining outside the canonical Seven. *The Outlying Fells of Lakeland*, which appeared in 1974, was in some ways an obvious sequel to the initial series. It lacked their magic, however, partly because the subject hills

Pike Rigg Bothy

smillie

were widely dispersed rather than occupying a well-defined area, partly because these fells were inevitably the last, minor sweepings of upland Cumbria. *The Outlying Fells* could be seen as Wainwright's budget-priced rarities and B-sides album: not without interest, but mainly for obsessive collectors and completionists.

The *Pennine Way Companion* (1968) and *A Coast to Coast Walk* (1973) are both discussed elsewhere in this book: they are probably the best-known post-Seven works, with the latter undoubtedly Wainwright's most influential later publication. The C2C route (not that Wainwright would have approved of trendy abbreviations) is now indelibly stamped on maps and perpetuated by guidebooks and—on the ground—forms his most enduring memorial not actually printed on paper (much more so than the rather artificial Wainwright Memorial Walk now being promoted in Lakeland). These two works also point the way for many of the subsequent books: in them we see Wainwright nosing cautiously out of the Lakes, trudging hesitantly through the Pennines and bravely setting out into at least a few small parts of the world beyond.

Wainwright eventually published quite a bit about the Pennines and the Dales, but he never attempted a complete Wainwrightisation of them on his Lakeland model. Nonetheless, *Walks on the Howgill Fells* and *Walks in Limestone Country* potter around in those strange lands east of Shap, and, taken with the relevant sections of *Pennine Way Companion* and *A Coast to Coast Walk*, allow Wainwright enthusiasts to explore large parts of the Backbone of England with the help of their favourite guide and guru. Compared with the Seven, though, the *Howgills* and *Limestone Country* volumes lack something. Curiously, something is missing partly because something has been added: photographs. Unlike the Seven, not everything in these books originated at the end of the great man's pen. Both books are also in the awkward landscape format which makes them annoying to shelve.

As the 1970s wore on, Wainwright's output became prodigious, almost amounting to mass production. Merely listing the works is laborious, so for a man well into retirement age the production of even largely forgotten tomes such as *A Furness Sketchbook* or *Three Westmorland Rivers* represents an impressive achievement. The *Lakeland Sketchbook* series developed into a further Lakes 'project', and in time *Lakeland Mountain Drawings* became a third.

Another new series took Wainwright outside England (at least in a publishing sense) for the first time. The *Scottish Mountain Drawings* books— amounting to six volumes issued between 1974 and 1979—offered the familiar pen-and-ink drawings, this time featuring the mountains of the country in which he chose to spend most of his holidays. Wainwright had remained such a local, Cumbrian-cum-Lakeland phenomenon that, until the appearance of these books, many Scots hillgoers had never heard of him. At that time I had never walked in the Lakes and I remember being puzzled by the appearance of these bulky, landscape-format works (is it becoming obvious that I dislike this shape of book?) alongside the more familiar works by Walter Poucher, Tom Weir, Hamish Brown and the Scottish Mountaineering Club. Who was this interloper?

Certainly, Wainwright seemed a little lost in the Highlands. Perhaps it was an area too large and diverse for him to conceptualise, resistant to the obvious divisions and categorisations of the small but beautifully-formed Lake District. Neither did Wainwright live on the doorstep of the Scottish hills and so he couldn't pack them into weekends spent rumbling mountain-wards in his beloved buses. He also struggled with the languages of Scotland, as shown when Hamish Brown, in his 1978 book *Hamish's Groats End Walk*, gently chided Wainwright for his complaint (in the foreword to Volume One of *Scottish Mountain Drawings*) about the complexity of Gaelic hill names. 'As regards pronunciation of Gaelic names,' Wainwright had written, 'the average visitor from south of the Border simply has to give up.'

In a 1979 interview, Wainwright told Hunter Davies (who would later become his biographer) that he wasn't much of a reader, not through any anti-intellectualism but as an unfortunate effect of cramming for his accountancy exams. 'Those years of killing study killed any reading instinct I ever had,' he said. 'I've hardly picked up a book since. I hate any sort of research.' Wainwright was probably exaggerating there. All those delectable little historical and folkloric gobbets in his books must have been picked up *somewhere*. In any case, Wainwright was too good a writer—wry, witty, idiosyncratic, precise—to have been the non-reader he portrayed himself as. A distaste for research is, however, suggested in those of his books that deal with furth of Lakeland—and the further away, the more it shows. To Davies, Wainwright admitted he was loath to begin his projected *Welsh Mountain Drawings* book because of his dislike of the Welsh accent. (The book eventually appeared in 1981, and was quickly followed by *A North Wales Sketchbook* and *A South Wales Sketchbook*: perhaps he found an interpreter.) The Lakes books were fuelled by love and reflected a deep affinity with and understanding of land and landscape. Perhaps there was too much of a deficit to overcome when dealing with other regions, a deficit that immersion in research material might have compensated for.

360° Panorama from Great Gable

In the 1980s, something strange stirred amongst Britain's veteran mountain gurus: they went mainstream, they burst into colour, they became public property. Poucher began to issue a jaw-dropping series of coffee-table books featuring his colour photographs, starting with *Scotland* in 1980. Some hill-lovers felt these lacked something compared with Poucher's earlier black-and-white classics such as *Highland Holiday*, but their evocative colour (and the occasional classic cars seen in the foreground) suggested the 1950s of cheery British Transport Films. With the reclusive, mildly misanthropic Wainwright, something similar occurred. He suddenly turned up—benign, genial, pipe-smoking and in colour—on a nation's coffee tables and on their television screens. A series of lavish books emerged from 1984 onwards (*Fellwalking with Wainwright*, *Wainwright in Scotland* and *Wainwright's Favourite Lakeland Mountains* among them), with a commentary by Wainwright himself, a few of his drawings reproduced and decked out with colour photography by Derry Brabbs. Some of the books were linked to BBC2 programmes presented by Eric Robson—who these days is chairman of the Wainwright Society, and who devised the Wainwright Memorial Walk.

The notion of the secretive, technophobic mountain guru holding forth on nationwide television still seems about as likely as the Reverend Dr Ian Paisley throwing smooth moves at an Ibiza foam party. Yet there Wainwright was, responding to Robson's promptings, his slow-burning north-country rasp quite the furthest end of the spectrum from today's fast-gibbering Zoo-TV estuaroid presenters. His technique seemed to be to ignore the camera and simply reminisce at random, rather in the style of Jack Hargreaves (successful TV executive who posed as a rustic country expert on programmes such as *Out of Town*).

The series of extravagant colour books was a short-lived phenomenon, except in tourist shops in the Lakes, where cheaper editions of some of them can still be found. Nevertheless, together with the TV programmes, they helped bring the name of Wainwright to a more general, national audience, well beyond the fellwalking ghettoes of Grasmere and the like. They also had a valedictory air, giving an ageing and ailing Wainwright the chance to visit again places that he thought he had seen for the last time. The late-period *Ex-Fellwanderer*, published in 1987 to commemorate Wainwright's eightieth birthday, has a similar last-stop-before-Valhalla feel to it. It's a sobering thought that must affect all hillgoers: there will come a time when we are no longer able to visit the hills we love. Wainwright expressed this painful truth as well as anyone. 'I love the mountains of Lakeland,' he wrote in the posthumously published *Wainwright's Favourite Lakeland Mountains*. 'They have been good friends to me over a long life, always there when wanted, always reliable, always welcoming.'

Still he wasn't done, however. *Ex-Fellwanderer* was followed by *Fellwalking with a Camera* (1988), reproducing many of the black-and-white photographs of Lakeland that had formed the basis for the classic drawings in the Seven and later books. It's a lesser production: Wainwright's drawings seem to live more and say more than these fairly ordinary photographs. Which is not necessarily the same as saying that Wainwright was a great artist: he was a meticulous and evocative one, for sure. He was also an able and pleasing writer, again if not a great one. Where he triumphed was in merging his various skills—writing, drawing, description, handwriting, mapmaking—into a unity that became a work of art in itself. For each of the classic Seven *is* a work of art, a beautiful, original, bibliophile's joy.

The visitor to Glasgow can, in my view, obtain no better souvenir of the city than the Queen's Park Football Club away jersey, in the orange and blue colours of sponsors Barr's Irn Bru. It doesn't matter if the buyer doesn't like football: it's a unique, quirky memento that cannot be mistaken and could come from nowhere else. Similarly, the visitor to Cumbria should forget Skiddaw slate ornaments and ashtrays with pictures of Ashness Bridge. There is no better Lakeland memento than a volume of Wainwright's Seven—unless, that is, one buys the complete set. It doesn't matter if the visitor is not a hillgoer or a walker: Wainwright's classics *are* the Lake District, between two covers.

The best of What Alfred Did Next are those books that stick closest to the original formula: *Pennine Way Companion*, *A Coast to Coast Walk*, *The Outlying Fells*. The various sketchbooks, the mountain drawings collections, the colour coffee-table tomes as well as oddities like *Westmorland Heritage* and *Kendal in the Nineteenth Century* (the latter drawn from negatives on glass that were too fragile to reproduce as photographs) do not excite the reader as much because they did not excite Wainwright either.

Two final volumes deserve special mention,

however. Wainwright's work as an artist for Richard Adams' 1977 novel *The Plague Dogs* is perhaps less surprising than it might be, given the book's Lakeland setting and Wainwright's well-known interest in animal rights. (Adams, incidentally, was another sufferer from 'What next?' syndrome—although, unlike Rowling or Wainwright, he encountered this after his very first book. *Watership Down* had been such a publishing phenomenon that it proved, ultimately, quite impossible to emulate. In fact, *The Plague Dogs* was well-received and sold respectably—except by the standards of *Watership Down*.) The story concerns two dogs who escape from a vivisection laboratory in the Lake District. They journey across and around the fells, their travels illustrated by Wainwright's sketch maps and drawings. In his preface, Adams wrote: 'I seriously doubt whether an author can ever have received more generous help and co-operation from an illustrator.' Yes, I know it *is* the sort of thing that authors write in prefaces, but it is easy to believe, given Wainwright's commitment to animal welfare.

The other notable example of What Alfred Did Next is *Walks from Ratty* (1978). This does not get the attention it deserves, being both slight (little more than a pamphlet) and of only local interest even within the Lakes. One detail that merits repeating is that it was Wainwright's first post-Seven work *not* published by the *Westmorland Gazette*, appearing instead under the imprint of the Ravenglass and Eskdale Railway Company. The little volume illustrates ten walks that can be taken using the Ravenglass railway and sees Wainwright returning to his beloved Lake District, to a specifically defined area, to the small page size of the classic Seven and to a mix of drawings, handwritten text and sketch maps with no photographs, colour or printer's type. It's a miniature gem (like the railway itself), the ideal souvenir of the splendid rattly journey from Ravenglass to Dalegarth.

I've used the words 'memento' and 'souvenir' a few times. Wainwright wrote many of his books so that he himself could use them to review, relive and recreate the walks and adventures he had undertaken in the past. His best works have the power to do this for all dedicated fellwalkers (who should, I might add, firmly shun the mock What Alfred Did Next products clogging up many a Lakeland gift shop— the Wainwright maps and notebooks and knick-knacks that besmirch his good name, just as tacky jewellery has conspired to sully the reputation of Charles Rennie Mackintosh).

It's not a comparison which the silence-loving Wainwright would have liked, but poring over the various post-Seven volumes is a bit like tracing the solo work of the Beatles after the break-up (and if you must have a link, did not Hunter Davies write the official biography of the Fab Four twenty-odd years before he tackled Wainwright?) In the flurry of Wainwright books published from the late 1960s to the 1980s, you'll find a lot of *Back Off Boogaloo*, rather too much *Mull of Kintyre* and a regrettable surfeit of *Got My Mind Set On You*. But, as I hope I've shown, you can also find *Maybe I'm Amazed*, *Instant Karma* and *My Sweet Lord*—if you're prepared to look for them.

Goat Crag & Skiddaw from the Fort.

A rather distinguished-looking genius
The man behind the Pictorial Guide

Thousands of people, entranced by his guidebooks, would have liked to have known Wainwright, to have been his friend, but Alf preferred to keep his own company. He was friendly with his cats—one of them often slept with him—and was so fond of most dumb animals, including dogs and sheep, that some people said he preferred them to human beings. But I hope he counted me among his few real friends. Certainly that was how I regarded him—awkward, shy and unsociable but friendly, genuine, straightforward and generous. Indeed, I have many reasons to be grateful for his generosity, which I will outline later. His colleagues at Kendal town hall—he became the town's borough treasurer—were, of course, better acquainted with him in his workaday life, but I don't think anybody knew him as well as I did in his real life, his outdoors life, between 1954 and 1966 when he was working on his remarkable *Pictorial Guide to the Lakeland Fells*. Two or three times we went out together on the fells. He didn't take me out: I took him.

🚬 🚬 🚬

I first met Alf in the late 1940s—probably in 1948 when he was promoted borough treasurer—although I had perhaps known him by sight from 1946 when I came to live in Kendal on demobilisation, as a lieutenant colonel, from the 14th Army in Burma. I was then covering the Lake District and beyond for an evening newspaper and lived in a stone-built house on Windermere road—the main road to Keswick. My front lawn sloped steeply down to the road and there was a bus stop just outside my garden gate. Years later I would often see Alf standing outside my gate on a Saturday or Sunday morning waiting for the Keswick bus. He must have travelled on this bus scores of times—on his way to explore the fells for his guidebooks.

Sometimes, if I was going on the fells myself, I would offer him a lift but he would never accept one. I think he really enjoyed travelling by bus although he couldn't be bothered chatting to other passengers. He just preferred his own company, looking out at the scenery. Often, too, I would offer him a lift home when I was driving back from my office for lunch—we then lived fairly close together, on opposite sides of Kendal Green—but, again, he preferred to walk home up the steepish House of Correction Hill. He took exactly one hour for his lunch, including the ten-minute walk each way. A very methodical person was our Alf. Incidentally, I always called him Alf. The 'AW' tag was, I think, an invention of the television people.

I was almost the only person to have accompanied Wainwright on his walks for his wonderful *Pictorial Guide*. I write 'almost' advisedly, for I now remember a Kendal bank manager who went out with him once or twice and, many years later, wrote to me about it. Apparently they had met on the Keswick bus and, surprisingly for Wainwright, must have chatted, realised they were going to the same fell and, even more surprising, Wainwright accepted his company on the hill. Months or even years later, they went out again and were sitting on Heron Pike on their way to Fairfield when Wainwright spotted me approaching from Nab Scar—I was probably doing the Fairfield horseshoe—and warned his companion: 'Look out, here's Harry Griffin coming. He talks too much. Let's

Great Rigg & Fairfield
from Heron Pike

Smillie

drop down to Alcock Tarn.' And they promptly dropped
down over the edge and I never even saw them that day.

This Wainwright observation about my garrulity
surprised me, for I never talk when walking uphill,
because of certain breathing problems. Indeed, the
ridge of Steel Fell, from Grasmere, is always known by
one friend, Ted Stacey, as the Ridge of Silence because
I once warned him, as we set off from its foot: 'You can
talk as much as you like, but you won't hear a word
from me.' And I wasn't aware that I said very much
going downhill or along the level, either, preferring to
enjoy the scenery. Wainwright, of course, hardly said
anything at any time in the fells, and never chatted,
but if he really felt something needed to be said he

would probably stop first. He didn't walk and talk. Alf was not a loquacious person at any time—except in his love letters, according to Hunter Davies in his biography many years later.

The first time I went into Wainwright's office to see him—perhaps I was writing a feature about the rates—he was studying some drawings, probably his own, on his desk, and hurriedly swept them into a drawer. Some time later the borough librarian, Harry Marshall, who was a close friend of mine, told me that Wainwright was writing a sort of a guidebook to the Lakeland hills and also doing the illustrations and maps. We would sometimes chat about it, the three of us. Later, Marshall became the publisher of the first Wainwright books, partly because Alf couldn't be bothered with all the clerical and wrapping work involved but also because he liked the name Henry Marshall—although Marshall was always known as Harry—and the address, Low Bridge, Kentmere, Westmorland. He thought the name and address added distinction and authenticity to the books.

Harry Marshall and I were both members of the Rotary Club of Kendal and each of us later became president. We were good friends and I tried to introduce him to rock climbing and, before then—after

I discovered the only mountain he had ever climbed was Vesuvius during his war service—to walking the fells. He had some difficulty with his first rock climb in Langdale and said this was because he had no sense of balance, having one blue eye and one brown one.

I also introduced Marshall's son, Roger, to climbing on the little crags near his Kentmere home and Roger later became a very expert climber. He emigrated to Canada and eventually was chosen to lead a Canadian expedition, which proved unsuccessful, to Everest. Much later, Roger decided to attempt a solo ascent of Everest by a particularly steep couloir that had been climbed by Americans, but perished somewhere below the summit. I don't think his body was ever found. When the *Westmorland Gazette* took over the publication of the guides, Harry Marshall lost the job and, until his death not many years later, always resented his treatment by Wainwright, who, he claimed, had never given him credit, or even proper thanks, for all his years of work.

Alf Wainwright was a tall, rather heavily built man with, in his later years, mutton-chop whiskers rather like Norman Nicholson, the Cumbrian poet who I also knew well. When compiling his earliest guides Wainwright didn't have mountain boots but wore ordinary town shoes. Nor did he have an anorak. He just wore an old lightweight mac and, of course, his flat cap.

An early walk with Wainwright was either along the Troutbeck fells or perhaps up the Tongue from Troutbeck Park. I can't now remember which or whether Alf had some particular reason for going there. We went in my car and eventually came to a wall over which I easily scrambled but Wainwright refused to follow. I pointed out to him that this was the easiest and shortest route and that if he didn't go this way he would have a long walk round. But he refused to follow. So I went on and waited for him, with increasing impatience, for about twenty minutes. 'I don't climb stone walls,' he said when he eventually caught up.

Another outing was when he asked me whether I would take him to Dove's Nest caves on Rosthwaite Fell near Glaramara. He was, I believe, studying that area for one of his guides and wanted to see the caves where I had often climbed. I think I took a torch and some candles. The caves are reached from Borrowdale by way of Comb Gill, and the entrance, where you need lights and some idea of what you're doing, is about twenty feet or so up the crag—a very easy scramble, hardly a scramble at all. My idea was for Wainwright to reach the entrance and possibly put his nose inside to see. No more. I would point out the climbs and we could then descend.

But as soon as Alf saw the simple scramble that a child could do he said, very emphatically, 'I'm not going up there!' However, knowing Alf's antipathy to rock, I had anticipated this, producing a rope I had secreted in my rucksack, but Alf recoiled from this as if it had been a poisonous snake. So, he never saw the caves and they are not described, in detail, in his guide.

Indeed, Wainwright was about the clumsiest mountaineer I have ever known, with little control over where he was putting his feet—despite the advice he gave to walkers in his books. For this reason—his lack of expertise—some of his lone, exploratory ascents—of, for instance, Jack's Rake on Pavey Ark or the front of Grasmoor, direct to Grasmoor End—were very plucky adventures indeed. Alf was a brave although indifferent mountaineer and it must have also taken courage to navigate across unknown hills, often in bad weather, without a compass. Alf never

Bass Lake
from Dodd summit

smillie

carried a compass and wouldn't have known what to do with one if he had. And the story of how he sought out, climbed and described all those remote hills, far from the Keswick or Borrowdale buses, has yet to be told.

For Alf never owned a car and could not drive, and it wasn't until after he had completed the seven volumes of his Lakeland *Pictorial Guide* and was working on other books, including his Pennine Way, Limestone Country and Howgill Fells volumes, that he was able to count on the services, as chauffeur, of the pretty, petite Betty, who had her own car. They were married in 1970 and lived together until Alf's death, at the age of 84, in 1991. Wainwright's first marriage had not been a success.

In truth, Alf Wainwright was a very remarkable, if unusual, man. Perhaps he was a genius. I said I would tell of his generosity. Two people were responsible for encouraging and persuading me to write, in 1960, my first of a dozen books. One was William Heaton Cooper, the painter, whose centenary was marked in 2003. The other was Alf Wainwright—both of them close friends. Alf went further, suggesting that he should advance me several hundred pounds to have the book published—he had the money then for his early guidebooks were selling very well—but I felt I couldn't possibly accept this generosity. I would have to find a publisher to take the risk—and eventually I did.

But Alf did much more than this for me. He specially drew for me a wonderfully accurate map of the Lake District, not reproduced elsewhere, for use as endpapers in my first book, *Inside the Real Lakeland*, and he also allowed me to reproduce several of his drawings in my early books. And, some time later, I asked him whether he would do, especially for me, a drawing of Dow Crag near Coniston where I had done so much of my early rock climbing. This he did very willingly—a splendidly evocative picture which, framed, had a central place in my drawing-room for many years. I promised a particular friend, a Wainwright fan who lives in Blackburn, that I would bequeath him this in my will but, recently, only too aware of my advancing years, I gave it to him, instead. People tell me the drawing, not reproduced in any Wainwright publication and quite unique, is worth at least £1000.

I didn't do as much for Wainwright as he did for me—he also dedicated one of his volumes of *Scottish Mountain Drawings* to me—although I did write the first published review of his first book, *The Eastern Fells*. This appeared in my weekly column, 'Leaves from a Lakeland Notebook', in my own paper, the *Lancashire Evening Post*, on 27 May 1955—the first-ever publicity for his guides that Wainwright received. I devoted nearly the whole of the leader page to this review, including the reproduction of several of his drawings. My review showered high praise on Wainwright—'the most remarkable book of its kind about the Lake District ever printed'—but I also included some slight criticism. 'I have already told the author,' I wrote, 'that he runs the risk of taking all the adventure, the joy of discovery, out of the fells by the very completeness of his work.'

I've never liked walking guidebooks to the over-familiar Lakeland hills, considering them unnecessary. Some simple hills have twenty books about them. A map is all you need. But, in his guides, Wainwright practically took people by the hand, destroying any sense of adventure. People carried them in their hand as they followed his instructions. Far better, I wrote, to use your map and compass, working out your own route and then read up your Wainwright later—to see what you might have missed. Alf knew my views on this—I often wrote about them when review-ing all his books or writing about him in my own books—and he would say: 'It's not my fault. I didn't expect them to sell so many.'

In my second book, *In Mountain Lakeland*, published in 1963, I wrote a chapter on Wainwright, describing him as 'a tall, well-built, middle-aged man, spectacled, grey-haired, rather distinguished-looking, with a long-ranging stride that covers the ground slowly but surely'. And Alf wrote to me complaining about one word in the description. He would have preferred the word 'rather' to have been omitted. In 1975, in *A Lakeland Notebook*, I included the first photograph of Wainwright ever published. It took me weeks of persuasion before he agreed.

I think Alf Wainwright probably *was* a genius, and I believe his best work, the work which is really his memorial, is the *Pictorial Guide to the Lakeland Fells*, which set standards that are unlikely ever to be surpassed. His industry—every evening, for years, working on his books—was awe-inspiring, his attention to detail unimaginable. He rewrote his first book so that each line finished at the end of a word, and he was quite incredibly single-minded. In my opinion, his mountain illustrations, ascent diagrams and maps were his finest work, of top professional quality, but he wrote quite well, too. Not so much in his guides but, for example, in *A Pennine Journey*, written in 1938 but not published until 1986. This, a full-length book about a walk to Hadrian's Wall and back by a different route from Settle, was the favourite book of my late partner, Josie—and of many other people interested in the great outdoors.

But, mostly, Alf Wainwright, brought up in a Lancashire mill town, really loved hill and mountain country and started to write, not to make money, but to get things down on paper so that he could relive his walks in old age when the hills were beyond him. 'And you don't want to be paid for writing love letters,' he wrote. And, when he did make a lot of money, he gave most of it away to provide shelter for lost cats and dogs.

Crummock Water & Grasmoor from Dodd

Dave Hewitt writes:

Harry Griffin died at the grand age of 93 during the preparation of this book, and will be much missed. He and I had corresponded over the previous few years, something that began following the death of his son Robin in 1998, just one of several close-family tragedies that afflicted Harry's later years. He was the most elegant of writers on the Lakeland fells—and on hills and mountains generally—and came from the old school where grammatical discipline, efficiency of style and pure natural talent had been honed via years of hard graft on newspapers. Think Neville Cardus on cricket; think Bernard Darwin on golf. Harry was in the same class.

We only met once, at his home in Kendal's Beast Banks. The house seemed too small for him, but this only added to the sense of it being a treasure trove, crammed with the bounty of a life devoted to words and hills. Harry—as I suspect was often his way—sat in his chair, glass in hand, and spouted all manner of interesting and entertaining theories about hills and the wider world. With his bright eyes and RAF moustache, he resembled the Major in Fawlty Towers—but of course I never told him this.

His beloved Josie was alive at the time, and she seemed a perfect foil: homely and practical alongside Harry's incurable-romantic whimsy. One anecdote concerning their banter must suffice. Harry was in full flow, slopping whisky out of its glass with the vigour of his conversation, and he gestured to the Wainwright picture mentioned in his piece here, a lovely large drawing of Dow Crag, hung above the fireplace. 'Of course, I knew Wainwright intimately,' Harry said. At which the voice of Josie drifted through from the next room, where she had been tidying dishes. 'I certainly hope not, Harry,' she said.

The wind fell from his sails, but only for a second or two. Lovely man.

Viv Cripps of Millrace adds:

And a kindly, courteous one. Our correspondence began late in 2003. Harry's letters were rather formal at first, so when he eventually addressed me as 'Dear Vivien (if I may be so bold)', I was disarmed. We talked about his new book on mountains and music, which Millrace agreed to publish, and we planned to meet. Alas, it never happened. On the day I heard of his death, a last letter arrived from him, dated 9 July and dictated from hospital. The shaky signature confirmed what he wrote: he was seriously ill but wanted to keep me up to date with the progress of his book. He was thoughtful and professional to the very end.

Online, on Catbells
Ushering Wainwright into the digital age

 In his work as borough treasurer in Kendal, Alfred Wainwright produced immaculately neat and accurate handwritten ledgers with a calligraphic skill and attention to detail reflected in his beautifully presented guides to the Lakeland fells. One cannot help but imagine that the very thought of a computer taking over his job would have horrified him, so it is interesting to speculate on what he might have thought about his books now being celebrated worldwide on the internet.

One wonders too what he would have made of his books giving rise to a list of fells which people actively seek to complete. These two things go together in a way, as the computer lends itself well to the manipulation of lists. Yet the concept of 'collecting' hills might well have seemed alien to Wainwright, just as it does to many who condemn the peak-bagging mentality and who feel that a hill should be climbed for its own sake rather than ticked off on a list. In truth, there is little difference. The hills are magnificent whatever one's motivation for ascending them, but the avid ticker will perhaps be more inclined to go out whatever the weather and thus suffer more while also experiencing those magical moments when the cloud clears to reveal a landscape much fresher and more dramatic than on a cloudless day. Or they might climb through the cloud and stand above it in sunshine, a situation more common than the fair-weather walker tends to realise.

Probably the first person to base a website entirely on Wainwright's fells was Paul Kennedy, who presented a diary of ascents that had been made in 1986 and 1987 (www.gillean.demon.co.uk). My own site, Mad About Mountains (www.madaboutmountains. com), started in quite a different way. I celebrated my retirement with a walk across Wales in 1993, visiting every 2000-foot summit. This used a list created by John and Anne Nuttall, with a strict drop criterion of fifteen metres giving a spread of 181 tops. Hence the walk became a south-to-north traverse of Wales as well as a peak-bagging exercise. I subsequently tried but failed to find a publisher for my expedition diary.

Then a friend suggested that I publish it on the internet—and so Mad About Mountains was born. The Welsh traverse soon became just a subset of this larger endeavour, which also recorded some of the significant mountains I had climbed around the world.

Then, in 1997, I acquired a digital camera. At first I wanted to use it as a webcam, training it on Skiddaw which stands within sight of my home. Soon, though, I realised it would be much more interesting to carry the camera with me wherever I went around the Lake District. Thus began one of the first websites which used a roving camera and which was updated almost daily.

Where does Wainwright come into all this? Well, when wandering the Lake District, one inevitably climbs 'his' fells, because almost every fell features in his books, and so it seems obvious to cross-reference

Blencathra: Castlerigg Stone Circle   smittie

the walks to the list. And once the list is there, it is obviously necessary to visit them all.

Nowadays it is easy to find dozens of similar sites on the web. A good starting-place is the online fellwalking club (www.uk.groups.yahoo.com/group/fellwalkingclub), a forum set up specifically to discuss fellwalking and concentrating mainly on those fells listed by Wainwright. Through this group I met and walked with other committed hillwalkers, for example Roger and Ann Hiley, who also have a Lakes-based website (www.hiley105.btinternet.co.uk), and who announced their intention to climb the last of their 214 Wainwrights on New Year's Eve 2001. So together we had a great outing to Lonscale Fell and Skiddaw, both of which the Hileys had climbed before but which could hardly be omitted on such a splendid day. Finally the champagne was opened on Skiddaw Little Man. Also enjoying that walk were Andrew Leaney and his wife Anne. Andrew's website (www.leaney.org) is probably the closest in concept to mine, featuring regular walks and summit panoramas. No surprise perhaps, since we own identical cameras, the Canon Ixus 400, which comes equipped with a special panorama mode and associated stitching software. Andrew's site is a good deal better organised than mine and concentrates almost exclusively on the Lakeland fells.

Meeting like-minded people for fellwalking is not something that would have pleased Wainwright; he is widely believed to have hidden behind rocks to avoid meeting other walkers. I too love walking alone, and have none of the hang-ups about solitary walking that spoil things for some women in particular. It is good, however, to meet fellow enthusiasts, so I am also active within Keswick Rambling Club, the best possible way of making friends in the town. (Wainwright helped to organise a walking club during his Blackburn years—the Pendle Club—but it appears they did not do a lot of fellwalking.)

The year 2004 marked the golden jubilee of the Keswick Rambling Club, and in what more perfect place could a club of this kind be centered? After all, in describing Walla Crag, Wainwright wrote of 'the pleasant Vale of Keswick, surely one of earth's sweetest landscapes'. Thus the club set itself the goal of climbing all 214 Wainwrights within the year. This was to take place via a combination of what have become known as 'A walks'—big outings such as the Kentmere horseshoe—and easier 'B walks' such as Walla Crag itself. This provided another great reason, an excuse perhaps (not that one was needed), to revisit every fell. So, for instance, there was suddenly a good reason to revisit Ling Fell, which Wainwright likened to 'a Christmas pudding'. Certainly not one of the most popular of fells, but on a spring day with the larks singing, with white fluffy clouds jostling with jet-black ones and with brilliant sunshine falling on fresh spring grass, it was an idyllic spot and the source of yet more atmospheric shots for the website.

The members of Keswick Rambling Club are now used to my habit of taking maybe a hundred pictures on a walk and sometimes lagging behind the group to obtain a panorama free of irritating moving bodies. They are tolerant of appearing on my site, although not always cooperative in terms of spreading out neatly over the hillside rather than of walking in an unphotogenic bunch. One member, Hilda Eastwood, particularly welcomes an appearance on my pages, and I have to be sure to include her in at least one picture each time so that her son in the USA can see where she has been. Like several of our members, she is still walking with us aged well over eighty.

Wainwright's selection of fells is certainly quirky. On the whole, however, especially if the outliers are included, every significant hill is visited. And of course some insignificant ones, too—Middle Dodd on the west side of the Kirkstone Pass being a good example. As one approaches from the north, Middle Dodd appears as a major mountain. But scaling its forbiddingly steep north ridge brings a top with virtually no separation from its parent fell Red Screes. Its neighbour across the Caiston Glen, High Hartsop Dodd, is almost as steep and even more deceptive, as the drop before the continuation to Little Hart Fell measures less than a handful of metres. Yet one can argue that Wainwright's selection of fells that *look* significant leads, overall, to a better list than does a simple drop-criterion selection such as the Welsh Nuttalls.

Middle Dodd ranks high amongst my list of frustrating fells. It remains the only eastern fell outstanding in the latest project for the website: to obtain a 360-degree panorama from every Wainwright summit. Several visits have always found Middle Dodd in cloud, the latest in driving snow as well. Of course shortcomings in terms of lack of drop ensure that on some fells such a panorama would be only partial anyway, with much of the distant view being blocked by the parent fell. But frustrating experiences such as those on Middle Dodd make me appreciate

Dodd, Longside Edge & Skiddaw from Little Man

all the more Wainwright's persistence and diligence, since he produced a fell-panorama from each of his 214 summits. Indeed, on Raven Crag above Thirlmere he rejoiced in the relief afforded 'the conscientious chronicler of summit views' by the screen of trees, and replaced the western half of the view with a rare self-portrait, albeit a view of his back.

It would be sad indeed if the proliferation of websites, some offering details of the climbs, caused the next generation of walkers to forgo the books themselves, for Wainwright's seven-volume *Pictorial Guide* is far more than a mere list of hills. His descriptions add an extra dimension—the direct ascent of Grasmoor from Lanthwaite Green, for example, being 'probably less difficult than the North Wall of the Eiger'. Can anyone who has read this then look at the impressive face of Grasmoor End in quite the same way again?

When my own set of panoramas is complete, and once 2004 has perhaps seen me again stand on every summit, I must seek some further project. It's not that I don't enjoy climbing the fells for their own sake, but my records show that I am more likely to go up handy Catbells once again than wander further afield—a good thing in some ways, but it's a pity to notice that I have not climbed Lingmell in this millennium. One idea might be to tackle every route in each of the seven books—although one or two of these are no longer available. For example, the ascent of Burnbank Fell from Lamplugh reaches the open fell by way of a track which is not a right of way and which is guarded by a hostile farmer. Some walkers attempting the west ridge of Great Borne report having been assaulted by a landowner grimly determined to assert his right to deny the crossing of his field between a bridleway and the open fell. Great Borne, incidentally, is a fell where, most unusually, Wainwright missed one of the best ways up: via Rake Beck.

New trees are another hazard, and the direct ascent of Low Fell from Loweswater is now virtually impossible. Conversely Dodd, beside Bassenthwaite Lake, has been completely transformed by partial felling, the provision of good paths and a waymarked route to the summit, which now provides that 'simply glorious' view denied to Wainwright by *pinus mugo*. Wainwright himself admitted that the books would become rapidly out of date as regards paths and fences, whereas the hills, especially the summits, would remain the same. Moreover, he included a few of the routes primarily as a recommendation to one's worst enemy—and having attempted and abandoned the ascent of Blencathra via Doddick Gill, I can fully endorse this route as being particularly suited for the purpose.

What a magical thing is a digital camera. I have to admit that I am totally in love with mine. No need to lie idly on the couch invoking that inward eye to revisit the dancing daffodils: there they are, dancing on the screen of the computer. The storm through which we struggled this morning, literally crawling to the summit cairn, is frozen now in manic distortions of walkers leaning into the gale at impossible angles. And although I might climb Catbells a hundred times, there is one place, one moment, which always commands a stop, a point where the perfect combination of ridge and sky leads the eye into the perfect landscape picture, of Keswick on Derwentwater backed by its guardian mountain Skiddaw, begging to be encapsulated in pixels. Every time I take this picture, the result is different. One day the lake lies below a sea of cloud with Skiddaw clear and bright above. Another day the mountain carries the cloud, lying across its broad back like a tablecloth with Keswick a miniature Cape Town. Or perhaps rain is lashing the hill and only the vague, hunched ghosts of masochistic ramblers loom from the mist and pass with a muttered greeting—although this scenario is, for me, unlikely because the massive privilege of living just ten minutes from the foot of Catbells means there is little motivation to scale it in inclement weather.

Returning home in the evening and being able to instantly relive the day via photographs is an amazing experience. It is easy to understand how Wainwright locked himself away every evening as a means of returning, in his case by way of pen and paper, to the beloved hills. Sitting at the computer, selecting the pictures that best encompass the day just over, I feel a true rapport with the master. Sometimes there is a conflict between selection of the best shots and trying to cover the whole progress of a walk, especially when half the day has been spent up in the clouds and the evening has brought sudden sunshine. Unlike the black-and-white sketches used by Wainwright, my photographs are crucially dependent on the light. Not brilliant unbroken sunshine, but a black sky as evening light floods the fells, with maybe a rainbow, the same carefully composed shot with the same tree framing the same summit, the same boat moored in the bay and carefully placed one-third of the way across the picture. And yet yesterday, today, tomorrow, each reveals different worlds of sun and rain, spring and autumn, calm and storm.

Rereading Wainwright's guides—not the descriptions of the fells, which are a constant source of inspiration, but the Personal Notes in Conclusion—I sense a current of sadness running through the series. Each area was so loved for two years but was then perhaps never to be revisited, as he says on the completion of his fourth book, *The Southern Fells*. This same feeling has always haunted the fells for me. During the few years before my retirement, I was visiting the district irregularly and wrote a set of poems of loss and longing

Catbells   Smillie

that are to be found on my website. Now that I have the good luck to live here I can climb a hill every day—and although this has in no way diminished their beauty, the pain of leaving is happily a thing of the past. There is still an underlying melancholy however, especially in the evenings and most of all perhaps beyond the summer solstice, a moment which has always filled me with the strongest pain of all, the pain of time passing and of long summer evenings declining into the short stormy days of winter.

For Wainwright, because he depended on buses for his transport, it seems that the fells were largely closed to him in winter—a sad thing, for the hills are at their most beautiful with a touch of snow. Nowadays, too, that great lover of solitude would surely have deplored the crowds which throng the hills from Easter onward. He would have sought out the quietest times, although at any time of year now it is not easy to walk all day and meet no one—as he did for two whole summers at the back of Skiddaw in 1960 and 1961.

During the years when Wainwright was creating his books, it seems that summer weekends were invariably spent on the fells whatever the weather. Only on the very last fell climbed as part of his 'fieldwork' for the last book (Starling Dodd, climbed on 10 September 1965), does he hint at problems caused by bad weather, especially in seeing and recording the summit panoramas. Then his winter evenings were spent in the painstaking task of recreating the fells on paper. My own pattern is very different. Although I cannot claim to climb a fell every day regardless of conditions, I do usually go *somewhere*—and, in the Lake District, a low-level walk, be it around a lake or along a valley, can yield almost as much beauty and interest as the ascent of a fell. Many would say that the valleys are even more delightful, but as somebody mad about mountains I could not possibly admit such heresy. Anyway, the evening's occupation is to transfer the best pictures on to the internet, a task which I feel sure gives me equal pleasure to that which Wainwright obtained during long winter evenings spent drawing them with such care and excellence.

Despite the crowds, the erosion, the footpaths restored sometimes unsympathetically (and in ways that would have appalled Wainwright), the basic beauty of the fells remains constant. As he said in the final book of his seven-volume masterpiece, 'the fleeting hour of life of those who love the hills is quickly spent, but the hills are eternal.'

About the contributors

High Raise High Street

Dave Hewitt has, since 1991, grappled with and generally overseen *The Angry Corrie*, the first and finest Scottish hillzine. In terms of proper jobs, he started as a statistician, strayed into social work, and now seems to earn money via dull bits of computer-related work. He finds that being absurdly tall helps in some aspects of hillgoing (yomping across moors, keeping an eye out for stroppy keepers) and hinders in others (wobbling along narrow ridges, weaving through twiggy gaps in sitka plantations). On the whole, he is happy with his lot.

W R (Bill) Mitchell was born in Skipton and still lives in North Yorkshire. He has worked in journalism for more than sixty years, having edited both *Dalesman* and *Cumbria* magazines, the latter from 1951 to 1988. He has written over a hundred books, including *After You, Mr Wainwright* (1992), subtitled 'Remembrances of the master of fell-walking'. In 1996 he was awarded an honorary doctorate by Bradford University, and he has donated an archive of books and papers to the J B Priestley Library at the university.

Val Hamilton has a degree in Japanese and linguistics, a postgraduate qualification in librarianship and has written a Master's thesis on the history of mountaineering in Japan. She has worked at Sheffield, Stirling, Glasgow and Strathclyde universities and is out in the hills every weekend, usually walking but also ski-touring on the rare occasions when it is possible in Scotland these days.

Ronald Turnbull is an all-weather walker, writer and photographer based in southern Scotland. He likes to sleep out without a tent on hilltops, and has achieved comfortable nights on sixteen Wainwrights and in two Lakeland caves. He completed the Bob Graham Round of forty-two Lakeland summits in 1994. Among his books, *Long Days in Lakeland* was highly commended in the Lakeland Book of the Year Awards 1999, and his guide to Wainwright's coast-to-coast route won the 1999 Outdoor Writers' Guild/Cola best guidebook award.

Graham Wilson was born in Birkenhead in 1939, where he lived, apart from a slight altercation with the Luftwaffe, until 1947. He moved to Sunderland, land of football legend, and once had his hair cut by Len Shackleton. He trained as a solicitor but made what would now be known as a career move, in fact a stab in the dark, into teaching, becoming head of English at the King's School, Macclesfield. His books for Millrace include *Climbing Down* (2003) and *Macc and Other Islands* (2004).

Robin N Campbell has held various offices in the Scottish Mountaineering Club and is currently its Honorary Archivist. His interest in mountain drawings dates from the graduation of his last daughter, when he found himself with money to spend and proceeded to waste it on buying old drawings. In a famous disagreement about the merits of photographs and drawings as mountain illustrations, Norman Collie and the artist Colin Phillip waited in the rain for the one train at opposite ends of the Kingshouse station platform. Campbell would have stood alongside Phillip, and Wainwright would have stood there too.

David McVey is a lecturer at the University of Paisley's Centre for Learning and Teaching. He has published over fifty short stories and hundreds of non-fiction articles on subjects ranging from acne to Scottish nationalism. His outdoor writing includes articles on the Lake District published in *The Herald*, *Cumbria* and elsewhere. His ambitions are to complete a novel, to avoid climbing all the Munros and to live to see Kirkintilloch Rob Roy FC win the Scottish Junior Cup.

A Harry Griffin was born on Merseyside in 1911 but grew up in Barrow-in-Furness, from where began a life-long (and career-long) love of the Lakeland fells. His journalism appeared in a variety of newspapers, most famously *The Manchester Guardian*, which in due course became *The Guardian* and to which he contributed a fortnightly country diary for a record-breaking fifty-three years. He was an excellent climber and skier as well as a walker, and he wrote a dozen hill-related books, from *Inside the Real Lakeland* in 1961 to *The Coniston Tigers* in 2000. He died aged 93 in July 2004. (See also page 140.)

Ann Bowker retired to the Lake District from a job teaching computer studies in Nottingham, thus fulfilling a long-held dream. She started a website which, with the acquisition of a digital camera well before they became ubiquitous, was soon carrying almost daily pictures of walks in the Lake District. Mountain walking was not confined to the Lakes, however. She and husband Rowland have climbed hills all over the world and, as the website title proclaims, are truly 'mad about mountains'.

**Craig Smillie** is best known to the hill community as 'The Swan', graphic creator of *The Angry Corrie*'s hapless hero Murdo Munro. Craig rarely ventures higher than a hundred metres these days, claiming he 'no longer has the poop for it'; but he illustrates items such as trig points, Trangia stoves and Rohan trousers from descriptions given by Murdo collaborator Perkin Warbeck. A fan of painting, rock'n'roll music and postmodern Continental philosophy, he lives on the south side of Glasgow and cites as influences Turner, Foucault and Keith Richards.

Index